Bullying in Sports

A GUIDE TO IDENTIFYING
THE INJURIES WE DON'T SEE

RANDY NATHAN, MSW

Pearson Learning Solutions, 501 Boylston Street, Suite 900, Boston, MA 02116
A Pearson Education Company
www.pearsoned.com

Printed in the United States of America

1 2 3 4 5 6 7 8 9 10 V0CR 18 17 16 15 14

000200010271847950

JH/VP

ISBN 10: 1-269-59385-4
ISBN 13: 978-1-269-59385-4

TABLE OF CONTENTS

DEDICATION

In memory of Mark Ryan Nathan
(June 9, 1971 – March 20, 2005)

Through his death he taught me the purpose of life

To my family

For showing me the true meaning of unconditional love

ACKNOWLEDGMENTS

This book began in March 2005, following the unexpected passing of my younger brother Mark. I would like to thank a number of people who were essential partners in this process. Please forgive me for all those who have been with me over the years who I forgot to mention.

I would first like to thank those who helped me with the *game plan*. Jay Dugan of the Educational Information & Resource Center, for believing in me by sending me to the Olweus Bullying Prevention Program to become a certified trainer. David Nash of the New Jersey Principals & Supervisors Association for being the first to allow me to present "Bullying in Sports" to educators and coaches in New Jersey. Lynn Lonsway with the International Bullying Prevention Association for my first national presentation of "Bullying in Sports: The Injuries We Don't See." And the 50+ people who donated over $4600 to my GoFundMe page to support my marketing and PR efforts. In particular, Mitch Slater, Laura Ziegert, Nile, Annie & Darryl Godfrey, Lenore Whitmore, Michelle Rennert (my loving mother-in-law), Elaine Wolfe (who told me to go out and live my dream), and Larry Nathan (my supportive father). My mother Sheryl Wolf whose memory has been ever present throughout this process. I know you would be so proud.

I would like to express my appreciation to those who helped me get started *down the field*. David Avrin, the Visibility Coach, for offering your expertise in getting my proposal to a place where publishers would be willing to consider this book. Traci Totino of TNT Educational Services for stopping me mid-sentence during the first three minutes of our intro lunch and texting LeeAnne Fisher at Pearson Education. Sherri & Perry Gold with the Sports Education Expo for connecting me with so many individuals.

I would like to express my gratitude to the many people who helped me get *over the goal line*. Marty Teller and Tom Chesson of the Sports Authority for creating an incredible opportunity. Photographer Johanna Resnick Rosen for making me look professional. The incredible people at Pearson: LeeAnne Fisher for being so proud to be a part of this book. Abe Chang,

John Wannemacher, Sara Cameron, Karen Whitehouse, and Richard Gomes for working so hard on this important work. Gary Adair for your creative vision for the cover of the book. Marta Justak for being my amazing editor. Thank you for pushing me to write, re-write, and re-write again, then polishing this manuscript to ensure the written message that goes out is communicated with the same passion as when I speak.

This book would never have been possible without the support and encouragement of those who cheered me on throughout *the game*. Jason Hartelius who allowed me to become Fox 5 Good Day NY's area Sports Bullying Expert. Mark Reisenberg, my spiritual and zen master. Mark Rizzi for allowing me to be the mental training/life coach for the Rutgers-Newark baseball team. Shyam Bhoraniya, my graduate intern and guru.

I also want to thank the following people: David, Laurie and Paul Keith (z"l), Melissa, Mira and Matthew Nathan, Rebecca and Jordan Lateiner, Michelle and Adam Shandler, Ellie Linder and Larry Lateiner, Rabbi Alan Silverstein, Rabbi Dan Levin, Rabbi Randi Musnitsky, Rabbi Ron Kaplan, Jonah Kaplan, Rafe Kaplan, Susan Werk, Meredith Murphy, Lindsay D'Ambola, Alex Tarris, Chris Kluwe, Tony Hill, Hollis Thomas, Diane Thomson, Lucinda Mejdell, Joel Burgos, Jason Burgos, Justin Gerardo, Sam Hart, and Lee Rosenfield.

I also wanted to thank the members of *my team*. To my four beautiful children Jessica, Alex, Mikayla, and Brianna. Your vitality in my life gives me strength each day to continue to chase my dreams to make this world a better place. You are the best children a dad could hope for: happy, loving and fun to be with—I love watching you play. Team Captain and wife Jessa (my angel). You came into my life when I needed you the most. You are everything to me and I cannot fathom my life without you. I love you, me.

And lastly thank *you* for reading this book. The change that needs to take place within the culture of sports is vast and cannot be done by one person alone. Together we will transform the world of sports, making it a place where our athletes can play and compete in a healthy, sensible environment.

ABOUT THE AUTHOR

Randy Nathan, MSW, (aka Coach Randy) has worked with thousands of youth, teens, parents, and professionals to help create better lives. He is the President/CEO of Project NextGen, a leadership, training, and professional coaching organization. Having earned his BA from the University of Colorado (Sociology & Education), an MSW from the University of Southern California, an MA in Non-Profit Management from Hebrew Union College, and his coaching certification from iPEC Coaching, Randy has spent over twenty years inspiring individuals as a motivational speaker, edutainer, athletic coach, camp director, professional coach, and now published author. Coach Randy is a Sports Bully Expert who has worked with countless individuals who have been bullied, as well as those who bully.

Coach Randy has coached baseball and softball at the recreational, travel, middle, and high school levels. He is currently the Mental Training/ Life Coach for the University of Rutgers-Newark baseball team. He has met individuals who consider themselves a "chew toy" for other athletes, parents who are distraught and frustrated with their school's or coach's lack of action, athletes whose parents embarrass them on the field, and the inability of coaches to comprehend their behavior towards players, officials, and parents both on and off the field. His high energy and dynamic approach engages individuals by introducing valuable strategies to overcome obstacles and inspires them to achieve their full potential.

Randy Nathan grew up in Denver, Colorado and currently resides in West Orange, New Jersey along with his wife, Jessa and four kids, Jessica, Alex, Mikayla, and Brianna.

Coach Randy provides keynote presentations and workshop trainings on bullying in sports, leadership, mental preparation, motivation, and other pertinent topics. He is looking for collaborative partners as well as opportunities to engage in the healthy growth of our youth. He can be reached by visiting www.bullyinginsports.com or coachrandy@coachrandysays.com. You can also follow him on Twitter @coachrandysays, facebook.com/coachrandysays and linkedin.com/coachrandy.

INTRODUCTION

Bullying is everywhere—in our schools, our streets, and our corporations. But in the world of sports, bullying rules.

You only have to turn on the news to see the heightened attention focused on the issue of bullying. Experts agree that bullying is a national epidemic that impacts hundreds of thousands of people across the country. The issue of bullying transcends all ethnic groups and social strata; however, there is a breeding ground for what is transpiring. It occurs under the pretext of sportsmanship and pushing for excellence. It takes place in the open, fostered in our culture and cheered on by fans. Bullying is born in the locker room. It is promoted on the practice field and the weight room. In sports, bullying is tolerated, supported, and often role modeled. The athlete is worshiped as a hero. The lip service paid to this national tragedy has allowed the problem to fester for generations. It is a source for the strongest to turn and use their strength on the weakest. This revered "hero" lives within an entirely different set of rules.

There are undeniable highlights that sports generate in our culture. The memories that are created span lifetimes. Some of the greatest feats ever achieved have come through sports. They offer inspiration and create life lessons about how to overcome adversity. Yet, through all the great elements that sports promote, they are also about winning at all costs and taking advantage of the weak. Athletes learn this mindset and transfer it onto their peers. It is about a culture that spills into the cafeteria, gym classes, hallways, and bathrooms.

This book is a wake-up call and shows that this silent crisis has existed for decades. The unspoken words within sports that drive this behavior are revealed. The current mindset that promotes intimidation is addressed. The book focuses on players who are pushed to play with injuries and calls out the homophobic environment that exists. It recognizes the hazing rituals that are passed off as traditions. This book is divided into three parts that explore the dark corners of sports and how bullies are created and encouraged by sports and why. Part I, "Get the Ball Rolling," discusses the elements within sports that create bullying behavior. Part II, "Play by Play," identifies the bullies in sports and how they torment their targets. Part III, "Game Time," offers a paradigm shift where sports can be used as a gateway for addressing and reducing bullying. Throughout the chapters, you'll find profiles of athletes who have dealt with bullying; statistics that support and substantiate positions presented in the chapter text, as well as charts, graphs, and tables; strategies and tactics for combatting bullying at the end of the chapters; additionally, sprinkled throughout the text, you'll find sidebars with tangential topical information.

Next to school, sports are the largest activity in which youth spend their time. One of the key predictors of popularity for males in high school is involvement with sports, validating why those who are successful in sports often get treated differently. Sports can create an attitude of haves and have-nots, which constructs the breeding ground for bullying and a culture with limited checks and balances. Players, coaches, and parents are each involved without necessarily realizing their particular role within bullying. Players treat their peers with a sense of entitlement while coaches focus on winning at all costs. Players can be dismissed. Coaches can get fired. However, the group that seems to have no accountability is parents. It is time to wake up. Avoidance is no longer an option, given the severity of what takes place throughout the country.

It is unrealistic to expect that we can completely eradicate this behavior, but we must do what we can in order to reduce it. We have a responsibility to our children to raise our awareness. Bullying in sports has been around for generations, but that does not mean we must continue to accept what we know as being wrong.

There is a popular Jewish proverb that states, "You are not required to complete the work, but neither are you free to desist from it." Taking the time to read this book is just the first step.

CHAPTER 1

The Good, the Bad, and the Ugly

The spirit of sports gives each of us who participate an opportunity to be creative. Sports knows no sex, age, race, or religion. Sports give us all the ability to test ourselves mentally, physically, and emotionally in a way no other aspect of life can. For many of us who struggle with "fitting in" or our identity, sports gives us our first face of confidence. That first bit of confidence can be a gateway to many other great things!

—Dan O'Brien, Olympic Gold Medalist, Decathalon

The greatest component of sports has to be the memories it creates, as those memories are passed from parent to child, becoming the stories of legend over time. So each time a new game is played anywhere, anytime, there is always the possibility of *it* being "the one." The one that has the last-second touchdown. The one with the walk-off home run. The one where someone sets a world record. The one where spectators are present for that special moment in time. It becomes their story that needs to be told.

STATISTICALLY SPEAKING...

Research has shown that sports and physical activity can contribute positively to students' physical health, self-esteem, and sense of connectedness to their school. In addition, participating on an athletic team may provide academic benefits, both directly through school policies requiring athletes to maintain minimum GPAs and indirectly by strengthening students' identification with their school communities.[1]

Attendance at this "special" event carries an even greater weight. The memory begins the very minute it occurs—a memory that happens instantaneously yet lasts a lifetime. That memory is then shared from then on with anyone willing to listen about "that time when...." It *is* the moment when heroes are born.

In the early 1900s, the daily paper helped to create those memories. Take, for example, articles like, "Yankees Buy Ruth and Home Run Bat for Over $100,000" from the January 6, 1920 *World* paper or "Dodgers Purchase Robinson, First Negro in Modern Major League Baseball" from the April 11, 1947 *New York Times*. By the mid-1900s, radio and television changed the way those memories were told. Commentators began calling the games, thereby adding a flair for the dramatic, "The Giants win the pennant, the Giants win the pennant!" Because most people didn't attend the actual game, hearing it on the radio or watching it on TV made the memory become personal. The capability for the audience and listeners to mutually celebrate immediately became possible. People no longer had to physically attend an event to feel as if they were part of the game.

These memories are shared over and over again with friends and strangers alike. Arguments develop over the memories because some believe their story is more substantial or "correct" than others. Fights ensue with great passion about how their sport's moment is the "best ever." People want to talk about how their story changed that moment in time. Everyone has a story. Everyone has a memory to share. It is something that burns inside us, needing to be set free.

There are numerous moments in the past 150 years in which sports were celebrated. Anyone can offer his perspective of the top 10 moments in sports history—top 10 lists of the best quarterbacks, the best goalies, or the best teams are only a small sample of the numerous categories that can be debated. Sports etch their role in our culture with new memories being created constantly.

Some of the greatest sports memories that no one disputes are the 1980 Olympics USA Hockey Team's victory over the former Soviet Union; Jesse Owens winning four gold medals during the 1936 Olympics, dispelling the supremacy of the Nazi Aryan race; Jackie Robinson being signed by the Brooklyn Dodgers in April 1947; and Joe Namath guaranteeing his underdog AFL Jets would win Super Bowl III. Each of these events and so many others provide sports fans with some of the greatest memories of their lives.

MIRACLE ON ICE

On February 22, 1980, a young U.S. hockey team faced the invincible Soviet Union team. Thirteen days prior to this game, coach Herb Brooks arranged an exhibition where the Soviets destroyed the U.S. with a score of 10-3. The Soviet team was made up of grown men, who were some of the best players in the world. They had won the gold medal at the four previous Olympic games dating back to 1964. The U.S. team was a group of college players with only one player on the team with previous Olympic experience. They were boys among men. Prior to the game, Coach Brooks spoke to his team:

Great moments are born from great opportunity. And that's what you have here tonight, boys. That's what you have earned here tonight. One game. If we played 'em 10 times, they might win nine. But not this game. Not tonight. Tonight, we skate with 'em. Tonight, we stay with 'em, and we shut them down, because we can! Tonight, we are the greatest hockey team in the world. You were born to be hockey players, every one of you. You were meant to be here tonight. This is your time. Their time is done; it's over. I'm sick and tired of hearing about what a great hockey team the Soviets have. Screw 'em. This is your time! Now go out there and take it!

The U.S. team was down 3-2 at the end of the second period. However, by the end of the third period, the U.S. team was up 4-3 as commentator Al Michaels called one of the greatest memories in the history of sports broadcasting. "11 seconds, you've got 10 seconds, the countdown going on right now! Morrow up to Silk, five seconds left in the game. Do you believe in miracles? Yes! Unbelievable!" David beat Goliath. Those who were watching on TV can recall this memory in an instant, now referred to as the "miracle on ice."

AN ATHLETE'S STORY—JACKIE ROBINSON

Jackie Robinson, number 42, was a remarkable person. Although the individuals during that time realized the significance of what he contributed to our culture, it is only in the past few decades that we can truly appreciate his accomplishments. Jackie's ability to stare racism right in the eyes, dealing with the hate-mongers and physical violence, paved the road for thousands of athletes who followed. He came from humble beginnings and became the first player to break Major League Baseball's color barrier that segregated the sport for over 50 years. He pioneered the integration of professional athletics. Not only was it significant within baseball when he courageously challenged the deep roots of the racial divide, but the impact was felt throughout the North and South. What may have been a simple game with a bat and ball turned this country upside down by challenging the status quo.

Robinson continues to be an inspiration to fans and players alike. The number 42 (Jackie's number) is the only number retired throughout Major League Baseball. No other player will ever be allowed to wear that number again. The sport of baseball allowed the racial divide to be addressed. It was sport that changed our world in that moment.

The lessons of hard work were the focal point for the U.S. team and Jackie Robinson. The ability to persevere in the toughest of conditions gives all of us the ability to relate to these two stories, reminding us that with determination, practice, and a little bit of luck, anything is possible. Anyone can win on any given day.

DIRTY SECRETS OF SPORTS

There was a time when life seemed a lot simpler without the stressors of today. We refer to those times as the "good ole days." Baseball was the American pastime. Football was in its infancy with players wearing leather helmets. Soccer was only played in England, and a high school athlete's greatest achievement was being a three-sport letterman. The heroes in sports were role models. They were honorable men living an honest life. They wanted to win and worked hard to do so. They were hard-nosed people who took pride in their sport. Sure there were some who lived on the fringe, acting out while drinking and dancing, but the fans didn't seem to hold those choices against them. Athletes were allowed to live it up because they had earned that right.

In the old days, professional athletes would walk down the street shaking hands with fellow Americans and signing autographs for kids. They knew they were role models. Athletes were the type of people anyone would want to take home and introduce to their mother. They came across as solid citizens, who were always doing the right thing.

The tides always change in sports—and at some point, a shift occurred. Historians say it was subtle, but history will show otherwise. It is difficult to pinpoint an exact moment, but it occurred sometime during the last half of the twentieth century. The professional athlete maintained the hero status, but the honor in that role seemed to disintegrate. Money with large salaries became a primary focus, as sports offered anyone with talent the opportunity to make a significant livelihood.

Sports television became popular with around-the-clock coverage, highlighting all elements of athletics. Professional sports were first with the growth of football, baseball, basketball, and hockey. Next came college sports, which allowed teams across the country to gain visibility. Then high school sports became a target with teams receiving national coverage. Television even made poker games popular with the creation of the World Series of Poker ... who ever thought playing cards was a sport? Recently, television has focused on youth sports with the coverage of the Cal Ripken and Little League World Series. Twelve-year olds can become national heroes because they are able to throw and hit better than their peers.

Colleges have TV contracts that pay millions of dollars to showcase their schools in local markets. The NCAA (National Collegiate Athletic Association) is facing attacks for profiting off the backs of their players with lawsuits for student-athlete compensation. College players are now demanding salaries to play for their school. A free college education is no longer sufficient because the potential to cash in on the moment is possible. Professional leagues have billion-dollar TV contracts that generate million-dollar salary packages for the players and coaches. Parents notice these options and develop plans early in their young athlete's life. There is now a dark side to sports that infiltrates the culture and promotes varying degrees of negative behavior that would never be allowed within other areas of our culture. It impacts the memories that sports create and lays the foundation for future generations.

THREE KEY WAYS TO WIN

Effective coaches understand that success in sports requires winning. Winning generates dollars. Winning secures a financially stable livelihood for them, their families, and their teams.

Successful athletes also recognize this requirement. In order to receive the big salaries, being the best is no longer sufficient. Winning is a core component. Those people involved with sports understand that success requires three fundamental abilities: aggression, repetition, and an imbalance of power.

AGGRESSION

The first component in sports is the ability to be aggressive in nature. Those athletes who are physically the strongest increase their chances for a win. This element of winning seems to be pervasive in every level of sports. Regardless of an athlete's age, coaches focus aggressively on winning. Parents push their kids farther and harder by hiring personal position coaches early in their sports careers. Personal trainers work exclusively with specific types of athletes, offering programs that will generate a possible college scholarship.

HORMONES: THE HIDDEN DARK SIDE

The need to be physically bigger has opened the door in the past two decades for human growth hormones (HGH) and steroids. Professional athletes in the national spotlight have been accused and ostracized for their role in using these performance-enhancing drugs. Some experts say that cheating has always been prevalent in sports, yet what is currently transpiring seems to be the most serious offenses.

Adolescents are particularly susceptible to this drug use because it offers a quick way to become bigger and stronger. Plus, adolescents see their role models getting away with steroid use, so it makes sense for them to consider doing the same at their level. By being physically bigger, they get more looks from colleges that offer scholarships. Recently, several Major League Baseball players were suspended for their use of HGH. And Lance Armstrong, the most popular cyclist in the history of cycling, finally admitted his involvement with doping. He acknowledged his responsibility in taking performance-enhancing drugs and being a bully. The importance placed on this aggressive component has created an undercurrent that creates a dark spot in sports. The memories that are recalled might be used to condone cheating, encouraging others to copycat those choices.

REPETITION

The second component of success in sports is repetition. "Practice makes perfect" was a mantra decades ago. Now, the new mantra is "*perfect* practice makes perfect." If something is practiced over and over and it is not perfect, then the obvious outcome is imperfection.

The focus on repetition creates muscle memory that has been proven scientifically to be significant in gaining an added edge within sports. The constant push for perfection can also be viewed in the context of winning. The team with the most wins ends up in the victory circle at the end of the season. The more practice, the greater opportunity there is to raise the trophy in triumph. This repetition not only impacts the physical nature of sports, but directly correlates with the mental aspect as well.

Nearly all experts claim that success in sports breaks down into two categories: physical and mental. The best of the best are physically stronger. Yet when it comes to understanding the approach of a world-class elite athlete, the experts acknowledge that the breakdown is probably closer to 15% physical and 85% mental. Going to the gym, working out, and practicing on the field are only a small part of the blueprint for winning. The mental component far outweighs the physical.

The mental repetition starts early in a young athlete's life with messages from parents and coaches. Winning at all costs is the core of this mental approach. Those players who are gifted seem to receive preferential treatment from others. They are treated a bit differently because they can throw a tight spiral or come closest to the pin. They immediately rise to the top of the social strata and are allowed certain entitlements. They learn firsthand that popularity in school goes hand-in-hand with their athletic abilities: The better the athlete, the greater the chance for acceptance. This has a tremendous impact on the mental mindset of a young impressionable athlete.

A TALE OF PERFECTION

Author H. G. Bissinger in his book, *Friday Night Lights,* focused on a heroic football team in Odessa, Texas. The book was based on a true story that highlighted Coach Gary Gaines and the Permian Panthers. (This story was also made into a movie of the same title and directed by Peter Berg.)

Bissinger chronicled Coach Gaines's constant pushing of his players for perfection. Over the course of the season, the team had to overcome significant challenges. Yet, they never seemed to reach their mark of perfection. However, they did eke out enough victories to find themselves in the state championship game. In the movie version, the story came to a climactic end with the Permian Panthers just barely losing. Their hearts were broken, yet their sprits were lifted by the powerful lessons they had learned. As the end credits rolled, the audience learned that the following season Coach Gaines and his Permian Panthers were undefeated and did win the state championship...they finally achieved perfection.

CREATING AN IMBALANCE OF POWER

The final component to success in sports is creating an imbalance of power. Being aggressive is only effective with the ability to use that strength to overcome an opponent. There are two ways to effectively create this imbalance, physically and mentally. Science supports that physical edge, which is obtained by being bigger, stronger, and faster (survival of the fittest).

Typically, the physical appearance of an athlete is markedly different than people who are not athletes. This individual easily stands out from the crowd. Others befriend him for various reasons, but an underlying incentive is his size and skill. In the gym, he is admired for his brute strength, which is rewarded by his peers. In the locker room, comments are made that reinforce the positive nature of a large physical stature. Regardless of the sport, the individual with the greater strength tips the balance of power in his favor.

The mental aspect in this imbalance is just as significant as the physical, maybe even more so. If physical strength is relatively equal among opponents, then the piece that tips the scale is creating a mental advantage. Using intimidation tactics provide this needed edge. Whether it is through trash talking, eye black, or pre-game rituals, getting inside the head of the opponent is ideal. Coaches who have the ability to magnify an opponent's mental weakness can clear a path for their players to win. Even fans at events are encouraged to participate in this advantage by cheering at certain times to throw the other player off his game.

SPORTS AND BULLIES— MAKING THE CONNECTION

Ironically these three components—aggression, repetition, and an imbalance of power—are also the core ingredients of bullying behavior. As a sports culture, we are unintentionally creating bullies. Unfortunately, this kind of sports environment is now the accepted norm, but if we want to defeat bullying, we need to get away from this concept. We need to be aware that the core components we inspire in sports are also the same elements that foster an unhealthy bully culture.

The most commonly referred to definition of bullying is, "When a person is exposed to repeated, negative actions on the part of one or more other persons, and he or she has difficulty defending himself or herself.[2]" The Olweus Bullying Prevention Program agrees with the three major components: First, it is aggressive behavior. Second, bullying typically involves a pattern of unwanted behavior repeated over time. Finally, it involves an imbalance of power or strength.[3] There are many variations when it comes to defining bullying, yet these three elements are the core pieces that offer a universal understanding.

For example, an individual with aggressive behavior uses words and actions that are destructive. This person does not need to be physically larger than others, but is able to create an overly forceful approach that comes across as hurtful. There are two types of aggression: direct and indirect. Direct aggression involves words and actions that are directed toward an individual or group of people, while indirect aggression is used in a covert way. Comments or actions are not specifically directed toward a person, but they still have a negative impact on an individual or group. Spreading rumors is an example of indirect aggression. These rumors begin to take on a life of their own and eventually get back to the subject of the gossip.

Sports are designed to pit one player against another or one team against another. The words used in sports support assertive actions and dismiss those who are not willing to put forth their best efforts. Successful coaches pride themselves on their ability to push their players to the limit. They challenge them to raise the bar of excellence constantly when striving for superiority. It is the pure nature of competition that forces athletes to go after other teams or players in an aggressive fashion in order to win. The "win-at-all-costs" mentality exacerbates this aggression, setting in motion a culture that continually looks to be better and stronger than the competition.

A key component that often separates bullying behavior from other types of negative interactions is that it is repeated over time. Anyone who has experienced any type of bullying understands this piece personally. It seems to happen nearly every moment of every day with no end in sight. It sometimes starts out of nowhere and continues without ending. Some individuals are considered "provocative targets" and seem to attract bullies. These targets find themselves as the recipients of that type of repeated behavior. Many experts believe it is "learned" behavior that has taken root over the course of time. It may also be behavior that has developed as a result of family circumstances and types of parenting. However one thing is certain, regardless of how the bully develops the negative behavior, anyone who is at the receiving end can be damaged permanently.

Creating an imbalance of power is a tactic that is mastered by bullies. Once a bully establishes this sense of control with regard to power, it is easy to manipulate his target by utilizing fear. The bully conveys the message acknowledging his (her) strength and the consequences that will develop if anyone challenges it. It is not hard to create an imbalance of power—the bully only needs to manipulate the perceptions of others.

When people think about the stereotypical bully from our past, they often envision an individual who is physically larger than most of their peers. This person always seems to get away with the bullying behavior without consequences. No one is willing to stand up to the bully. This lack of confrontation reinforces the perception that the strongest control the weakest. However, bullying is not about size. It is about the ability to create an imbalance of power. As long as this imbalance exists, whether real or perceived, the bully will always get away with hurting others.

In sports, the most successful athletes must create an imbalance of power over their competition. In order to win championships, coaches have to put their players into a position of strength in order to identify their opponent's weaknesses. Once these deficiencies are realized, winning coaches are able to develop game plans that attack those weaknesses to increase their chances for victories. The primary goal within sports is to maximize that imbalance. Without it, teams cannot win. This is most clearly seen in professional sports. In baseball, there are teams with larger payrolls pitted against teams with smaller ones. In most circumstances, the teams with the larger payrolls are in a more powerful position because they can buy talent, although in the National Football League significant efforts have been made to create parity with a salary cap. The NFL's new strategy enables teams who may be on the losing end in one season to have the opportunity to be successful the following season. However, professional athletes know that the only way to continue their profession is to win. They adapt by doing what they can to develop an imbalance of power.

A real commitment is needed to help players, parents, and coaches understand how bullying is cultivated in sports. Awareness must be raised. Encouraging coaches and parents to recognize the overall error of their ways, and the environment they have supported these past several decades can do this.

Coaches at every level must take stock of their attitudes toward their players. They must be held accountable for their actions and recognize they can impact the memories they are creating for their players. Players must be led to renew the honor in sports and understand they are leaders in their schools and communities. Coaches must teach the players that their talent is appreciated on the field, but their skills are better served as a leader who supports those who cannot defend themselves off the field.

Sports will always create those incredible memories that are needed to sustain our dreams. Sports offer lessons about adversity, teamwork, and success. However, they also teach players to have a sense of entitlement and aggression. The sports arena allows parents to act unreasonably and promotes coaches who use their roles to create an imbalance of power. It is now a moral imperative to rethink our current structure, accepting the positives, while re-creating the negatives.

Sports can now be used as a gateway for intervention to prevent negative types of behavior. Coaches and parents can refocus on the honor and responsibilities that come with being an athlete. They can take the positive skills in sports and adapt them to everyday occurrences. They can get off the sidelines and into the game by becoming individuals who stand up to this type of negative, bullying behavior. Athletes can help foster cultures of acceptance in schools by changing the climate. Coaches can hold their players accountable to behavior unbecoming of a leader in their school. Athletes can be taught these lessons, which will provide opportunities for the future.

AN ATHLETE'S STORY—CARSON JONES[4]

Quarterback, Queen Creek High School Football
Queen Creek, AZ – December 2012

Carson Jones didn't think he was doing anything special when he asked his buddies on the Queen Creek high school football team in Queen Creek, Ariz., to help watch over a special-needs sophomore who was getting picked on by other students. The 18-year-old quarterback with a 4.3 GPA had no idea how his good deed would end up changing the life of Chy Johnson, whose neurological disorder limited her cognitive abilities to that of a third-grader. But Johnson, 16, went from being a bullied outcast to becoming one of the most celebrated kids at Queen Creek High.

Chy's mother Liz believed had it not been for Jones, she would have pulled Chy out of school and home schooled her. She first met Jones years earlier while working as a teacher's aide in his elementary school. When Chy started coming home from her classes in tears, describing how kids were throwing trash at her and calling her names, Liz wondered if maybe the "wholesome, good-natured" Jones might be able to help.

Liz tracked Jones down through his Facebook page and asked if he could find out who was picking on her daughter. The next day, Jones found Chy sitting alone in the cafeteria and asked her to come sit with him and a group of other seniors on the football team.

Chy started spending time with Jones and the other players. Simultaneously, Jones approached her tormentors to get them to leave her alone. Not only did the bullying stop, but the players also made Chy an unofficial member of their team—walking her to classes, taking her to dances and parties, even inviting her down to the sidelines during games.

Carson and the rest of the team's kindness hasn't been lost on Chy. "They're my boys and I'm their lucky girl," she says. "They're awesome."

STRATEGIES AND TACTICS: BULLY BASICS

- "A person is bullied when he or she is exposed, repeatedly and over time, to negative actions on the part of one or more other persons, and he or she has difficulty defending himself or herself."[5]

- It might be hard to tell the difference between playful teasing and bullying, but bullying is not teasing. Teasing usually involves two or more friends who act together in a way that seems fun to all the people involved. Often, people tease each other equally, but it never involves physical or emotional abuse.[6]

- Bullying is not conflict. Conflict generally involves some type of disagreement between two or more individuals. Even though it may be aggressive in nature, it does not involve an imbalance of power. The parties involved are able to defend their own perspective.

ENDNOTES

1 H. W. Marsh, S. Kleitman, "Extracurricular school activities: The good, the bad, and the nonlinear," *Harvard Educational Review*, 72(4), (2002), 464–514.

2 Dan Olweus, *Bullying at School: What We Know and What We Can Do* (Oxford, England: Blackwell Publishing, 1993).

3 Olweus Bullying Prevention Program.

4 http://www.people.com/people/article/0,,20656400,00.html

5 Olweus Bullying Prevention Program (from the training).

6 Ibid.

CHAPTER 2

The Culture of Bullying in Sports

I've worked too hard and too long to let anything stand in the way of my goals. I will not let my teammates down, and I will not let myself down.
—Mia Hamm, Professional Soccer Player

Imagine being in high school on a sunny morning in spring. Students are milling about the hallways headed to class. Friends give each other high-fives, laughing about the stories of recent happenings. The bell rings as the students settle into their seats. It is a regular day, just like all the others that preceded it. Students gather in the cafeteria, waiting in line for lunch. Out of nowhere, a popping sound is heard. Panic sets in as stunned onlookers discover two people dressed in black coats holding weapons, shooting, and moving toward the entrance of the school. Students run in all directions seeking cover from the gunfire. Shots are fired toward the soccer field, but no one is hit. Teachers get kids inside their rooms and hide under desks in silence.

Three minutes later, police respond to the scene, engaging in a gunfight with the two people in black coats. The shooters duck back into the school, walking through the hallways seeking specific individuals. They throw pipe bombs and fire at anyone they encounter. They move along the main entryway and head toward the library, calling for "all jocks wearing white hats." Students are locked in rooms with tears falling uncontrollably doing everything they can to stifle their sobbing while staying out of sight, praying not to be heard. The shooters make their way to the library, reload their weapons, and look for more students to kill.

For the next half hour, these two criminals wander the school building, firing guns and setting off bombs. As the first SWAT team enters the school, the two commit suicide—one by firing a shotgun through the roof of his mouth, the other by shooting himself in the left temple. The total death count is 12 students and 1 teacher, and 27 were injured. The bloodshed is over, but it forever changes the sanctity of the school environment.

April 20, 1999 went down in infamy as the date of one of the most horrific school shootings of all time. The two killers from Columbine High School went on a calculated rampage with the intent to murder innocent people. In the aftermath of what transpired, experts searched for a rationale to explain what happened. Issues of psychopathy and depression were initial considerations. Then came video games, social climate, and even music as possible causes. However, the area that seemed to develop the strongest link for why the tragedy occurred was bullying. Some stories claimed the two killers were victims of bullying for four years, and it seemed as if they were seeking out the jocks who had tormented them throughout high school. Others said that even though bullying was present in school, it was very unlikely that the shooters were victims of bullying. Unfortunately, the two murderers took their own lives with the real truth forever being buried with them. One thing is certain: What happened during that carnage drastically changed the way our society views bullying.

STATISTICALLY SPEAKING...

- In 12 of 15 school shooting cases in the 1990s, the shooters had a history of being bullied.[1]
- Two-thirds of students who are bullied report that the bullying happens in two or more locations.[2]
- Boys and girls are most often bullied at school in the lunchroom, hallways/stairwells, playground/athletic fields, and in class.[3]

THE LAWS CHANGE

Since the Columbine massacre, professionals around the country have become aware of their gross misunderstanding of bullying behavior. What was once considered long-established youthful behavior is now considered detrimental and destructive. The behavior of the bully has been studied afresh with the realization that bullying actions can cause victims lifelong harm. Victims are now viewed with greater compassion, and efforts have been focused on how to implement policies to protect potential victims and guard against bullying. Research has shown that a school's culture can be instrumental in the establishment of bullying behavior. The climate in school plays a vital role—whether or not it allows bullying behavior to become part of the expected norm. The culture can become a silent entity, sustaining bully behavior that is passed down to each new group of students.

Columbine demonstrated a powerful paradigm shift in the perception of bullying behavior. In order to preempt other "Columbines," states across the country began to draft legislation against potential bullying behavior. Students who were considered bullies began to face the consequences of their behavior. Victims were identified and offered appropriate intervention skills and counseling. Laws were put into place to ensure that this type of situation would never happen again. As of 2013, every state in the United States except for Montana has passed school anti-bullying legislation.

Programs like the Olweus Bullying Prevention Program were developed to assist schools in addressing their culture. Rules were created to provide school communities with a matrix that could be followed to create safe cultures for all students. Anti-bullying programs identified issues pertaining to bullies, victims, and bystanders. Common locations that offered a safe haven for bullies to humiliate targets were identified. Strategists started to recognize how schools could change their culture by creating an environment in which bullying was prohibited. In order to reduce bullying, an environment had to be created with a culture that encouraged positive behavior instead. Bullies were now put on notice that there *would* be consequences to their actions.

STATISTICALLY SPEAKING...

Cyberbullying is the fastest growing form of bullying, yet ranks as one of the least reported forms of bullying.[4]

- Over 80 percent of teens use a cell phone regularly, making it the most popular form of technology and a common medium for cyberbullying.
- About half of young people have experienced some form of cyberbullying, and 10 to 20 percent experience it regularly.
- Mean, hurtful comments and spreading rumors are the most common type of cyberbullying.
- Girls are at least as likely as boys to be cyberbullies or their victims.
- Boys are more likely to be threatened by cyberbullies than girls.
- Cyberbullying affects all races.
- Cyberbullying victims are more likely to have low self-esteem and to consider suicide.[5]

STATISTICALLY SPEAKING...

New bullying statistics for 2010 revealed that about one in seven students in kindergarten through 12th grade is either a bully or has been a victim of bullying.[6]

- Over half, about 56 percent, of all students have witnessed bullying take place while at school.

- A reported 15 percent of all students who don't show up for school report it to be out of fear of being bullied while at school.

- There are about 71 percent of students that report bullying as an ongoing problem.

- Along that same vein, about one out of every 10 students drops out or changes schools because of repeated bullying.

- One out of every 20 students has seen a student with a gun at school.

- Some of the top years for bullying include 4th through 8th graders in which 90 percent were reported as victims of some kind of bullying.

- Other recent bullying statistics reveal that 54 percent of students reported that witnessing physical abuse at home could lead to violence in school.

- Among students of all ages, homicide perpetrators were found to be twice as likely as homicide victims to have been bullied previously by their peers.

- There are about 282,000 students that are reportedly attacked in high schools throughout the nation each month.

BULLYING IN SPORTS

Bullying in sports exists for two prominent reasons. First, the overall culture within schools provides the foundation for the behavior. Second, that behavior is enabled through a separate culture within sports. Bring the two cultures together and bullying thrives.

Athletes have significant visibility in school. They are placed on a pedestal that comes with a "worship" mentality. Preferential treatment is the expected norm for athletes. Classmates want to be seen in the same social groups. Teachers give special consideration to them, often willing to "look the other way." Parents encourage their players to work hard to gain that unique status. Administrators provide opportunities for teams to be the center of attention where winning streaks, playoffs, and state rivals are concerned. The annual homecoming events in high schools and colleges are celebrated during the football season. Pep rallies are held, athletes are idolized, and the "big game" is the talk of the town. The following charts indicate the ubitquitous nature of sports in school settings for all grades and ages.

WHAT'S IN A GAME (2013)?[7]

Youth Sport Statistics (Ages 5-18)	Data
Number of kids who play organized sports each year	35 Million
Percent of kids who play sports outside of school	60%
Percent of boys who play organized sports	66%
Percent of girls who play organized sports	52%
Percent of coaches who are dads coaching their own kids	85%
Percent of corporation executives who played sports	73%

NUMBER OF KIDS WHO PLAY ON A TEAM BY AGE[8]

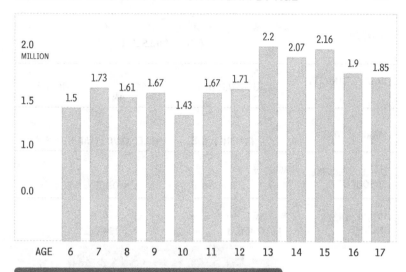

Chart reprinted by permission of *ESPN The Magazine*.
Data sourced from Sports & Fitness Industry Association.

STUDENTS WHO ARE INVOLVED IN AT LEAST ONE ORGANIZED SPORT

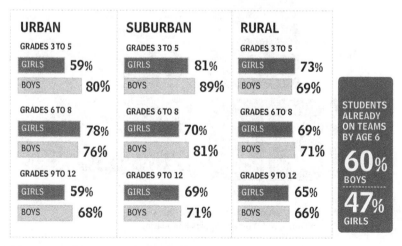

Chart reprinted by permission of *ESPN The Magazine*.
Data sourced from Don Sabo/ Women's Sports Foundation.

MEAN AGE AT ENTRY INTO ORGANIZED/TEAM SPORTS

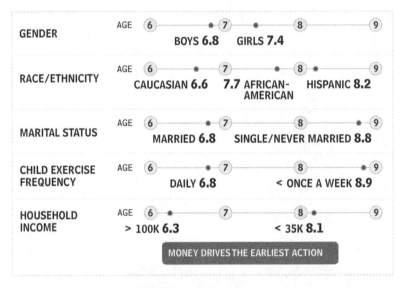

Chart reprinted by permission of *ESPN The Magazine*.
Data sourced from Don Sabo/ Women's Sports Foundation.

PERCENTAGE OF STUDENTS WHO SAY SPORTS ARE A BIG PART OF WHO THEY ARE

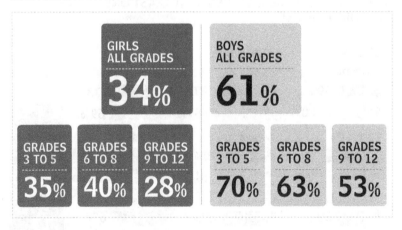

Chart reprinted by permission of *ESPN The Magazine*.
Data sourced from Don Sabo/ Women's Sports Foundation.

PERCENTAGE OF ADOLESCENTS WHO PLAY EACH SPORT

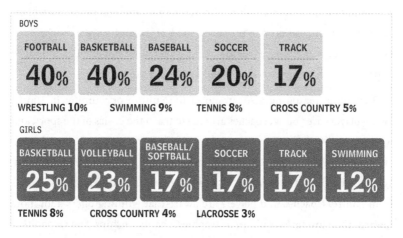

BOYS

FOOTBALL	BASKETBALL	BASEBALL	SOCCER	TRACK
40%	**40**%	**24**%	**20**%	**17**%

WRESTLING 10%   **SWIMMING 9**%   **TENNIS 8**%   **CROSS COUNTRY 5**%

GIRLS

BASKETBALL	VOLLEYBALL	BASEBALL/SOFTBALL	SOCCER	TRACK	SWIMMING
25%	**23**%	**17**%	**17**%	**17**%	**12**%

TENNIS 8%   **CROSS COUNTRY 4**%   **LACROSSE 3**%

Chart reprinted by permission of *ESPN The Magazine.*
Data sourced from Don Sabo/ United States Tennis Association.

Bullying in sports manifests itself with the support of everyone involved. It is encouraged and condoned by players. Coaches accept it. Parents promote it. Bullies exist in sports because all of the ingredients of bullying come together to create a perfect storm. The rules that go against the culture of bullying are ignored in sports because morality is suspended. Behavior that is unacceptable in the classroom becomes the norm on the field. It permits players to use their strength to focus on the less talented player. It allows coaches to use offensive words by screaming at players. It encourages parents who aggressively pace on the sidelines yelling at their daughter to play harder. A double standard exists with athletes given a pass because their behavior falls within the rubric of sports.

According to sports psychologist Brenda Bredemeier, "Adults and children tend to suspend their normal level of moral reasoning when entering the sporting arena and adopt a form of 'game reasoning' that allows them to be more willing to accept unethical and unsportsmanlike behavior simply because it is sport.⁹" At its core, the culture of game reasoning is the willingness to accept offensive behavior that occurs in sports, while condemning it if it is portrayed in other aspects of life. Teachers are not allowed to confront a student in class by grabbing the student's shirt, pulling him close, and screaming over his poor test skills. However, that same teacher puts a whistle around her neck, walks on to the soccer field, and calls herself a coach. She is now allowed, even encouraged, to scream at that same student. It is condoned as part of the learning that goes along with the sport.

That same reasoning also promotes the culture of winning in sports. When players are young, coaches are able to teach the basics of the sport, and winning is not their primary concern. They focus on the fundamentals with everyone being a winner. As athletes age, winning becomes more significant. Winning becomes the measure of what determines or differentiates success from failure. Coaches and players are aware that winning offers a lot more rewards than losing. Winning gets trophies, championships, and recognition in the press. As players move along the spectrum of sports from recreational sports to travel to high school to college, the increased focus on winning becomes embedded in the psyche of the bully culture. Winning provides opportunities for college scholarships, and for those select few who make it, seven-figure salaries.

Game reasoning also impacts other behaviors in sports. Comments such as "boys will be boys," they were just "roughhousing," or "it's just part of the game" are tossed around and provide excuses for actions that are considered harmful in other aspects of life. Adults in a supervising capacity allow their moral reasoning to be compromised because of the sports component. As athletes continue this inappropriate behavior, it eventually becomes the accepted norm. What is actually taking place is an authentic form of bullying.

In sports, the bully is allowed to reign supreme. On the field, players talk trash toward other players. There is name-calling based on sexual orientation. Baseball coaches are cheered as they run on the field screaming at an umpire. Parents sit together in the stands talking to one another and complaining about the coach. Fans cheer when two hockey players square off at one another, fighting until they hit the ice. It's all part of the game. The bully culture in sports becomes part of the norm.

We accept this culture without anyone standing up to it. Maybe it is fear. Maybe "game reasoning" is so significant that it is just not possible to recognize. However, athletes fall victim to the temptations of the popular status. A wake-up call must be provided to our role models. As long as the culture and "game reasoning" in sports go unchallenged, it will be difficult to address the bullying behavior that currently exists.

STRATEGIES AND TACTICS: BULLY CULTURE AND CLIMATE[10]

- Bullying can affect everyone—those who are bullied, those who bully, and those who witness bullying.

- Parents, school staff, and other adults in the community can help kids prevent bullying by talking about it, building a safe school environment, and creating a community-wide bullying prevention strategy.

- The best way to address bullying is to stop it before it starts.

- Community-wide strategies can help identify and support children who are bullied, redirect the behavior of children who bully, and change the attitudes of adults and youth who tolerate bullying behaviors in peer groups, schools, and communities.

- When adults respond quickly and consistently to bullying behavior, they send the message that it is not acceptable.

- The most effective tool to combat bullying is adult intervention.

ENDNOTES

1 http://www.stopbullying.gov/at-risk/effects/index.html

2 Joseph G. Kosciw, Ph.D., et al., *The 2011 National School Climate Survey: The experiences of lesbian, gay, bisexual and transgender youth in our nation's schools.* New York: GLSEN (2012).

3 Ibid.

4 Cyberbullying Research Center, http://www.bullyingstatistics.org/content/cyber-bullying-statistics.html

5 Ibid.

6 http://www.bullyingstatistics.org/content/bullying-statistics-2010.html

7 http://www.statisticbrain.com/youth-sports-statistics/

8 Sports and Fitness Industry Association (SFIA), *ESPN The Magazine,* http://espn.go.com/espn/story/_/id/9469252/hidden-demographics-youth-sports-espn-magazine

9 Bredemeier, B. J., and Shields, D. L., "Game reasoning and interactional morality." *Journal of Genetic Psychology,* 147, (1986b), 257-275.

10 www.stopbullying.gov

CHAPTER 3

The Locker Room Mentality

To be the man, you have to beat the man.
—Ric Flair, Professional Wrestler

Overall, there are incredible moments that are shared through sports. However, there are also great concerns. Professional sports are worshipped in the United States: NFL on Sundays, college football on Saturdays, the Super Bowl, the World Series, the Triple Crown, the World Cup, the Stanley Cup, the BCS, and March Madness all contribute to the fanaticism called sports. What was once a very small component of the daily news is now a multi-billion dollar industry. There are 24-hour sports networks offering up-to-date stories. Magazines and books are available that address all types of issues in sports. There are endless websites highlighting every corner of the sports world, giving anyone with access to the Internet a platform to offer his opinion. Individuals involved with sports are placed on pedestals by admiring fans. An unhealthy focus is created as sports figures are seen as the standard by which to set life goals and ambitions. Their lifestyles are seen as the ultimate way of life both in success and financial terms.

As with all issues pertaining to youth and teens, there are solid arguments on both sides of the fence regarding our society's involvement and infatuation with sports. The proponents of sports argue that sports offer opportunities for athletes to develop lifelong strategies that are not taught in the classroom. They believe sports teach team building, increase confidence and coping skills, and inherently provide important health advantages regarding physical fitness. Others also say sports help athletes develop healthier peer relationships and learn about responsibility and the importance of working with others. Coaches, in particular volunteer coaches, understand the role of sports and often choose to offer their time in this capacity because they also benefit from being involved with sports and want to pass on their knowledge of the game, as well as help shape the lives of young athletes.

The critics, while they do appreciate the importance of all the positive elements of sports, are openly concerned with the overwhelming focus on winning, the excess physical and psychological demands, the adult role (in particular the untrained) that often interferes with the "fun" of the game, and the year-round approach most competitive sports take in developing young athletes. The three-sport athlete is nearly obsolete because of the pressures being placed on parents and athletes to spend their time on one sport instead of enjoying and playing many sports. The school of thought is to invest in one sport and become the best that you can be—with the potential to increase the possibility of playing at the college or professional level. Given the current costs of a college education, it's no wonder parents decide to focus on sports to potentially help pay for school.

Anyone involved with sports goes through a process of significant preparation. It begins early in life, starting with a simple gift of a football or a softball glove when a child is young and naive. An innocent game of catch with a parent or uncle turns into registration for a recreational sports team. Then over a couple of years with interest in the sport building, the games start to get a bit more important. Players develop modest skills as competition begins to enter the sport. While the passion slowly develops, parents who previously barely watched the game now start watching and critiquing. The coach starts putting in only the best players, while the average kid sits on the bench. The mindset developing in the young athlete is about the importance of winning, as opposed to everything else. Winning becomes everything. The fact that it's just a game is no longer sufficient. It becomes everything to that person. However, the problem is that it's an artificial world. It isn't the real world.

In addition to these concerns, there is also a secret social order that indoctrinates athletes—a prominent component of sports where dominance and elitism are bred. It is the one place, regardless of background, where everyone on the team is on equal ground, fighting for a common cause. It is the locker room, and it is only available to those invited individuals who are permitted to enter. Anything done in this place is protected behind the cloaked shroud of brotherhood. Whatever is mentioned stays hidden by the sacredness of trust. The activities that take place in the locker room might be viewed by outsiders as abhorrent, yet they are deemed acceptable under the guise of a team. It is a revered setting that is envied by those who are not allowed to enter, yet retains a sense of privilege for those who have access.

In this environment, a particular mindset is communicated that dictates behavior. Players learn direct and subtle messages about what is expected of them. The locker room is a place where things are said without worrying about consequences. No outsiders are permitted. An invited member is required to go through an initiation process in order to be an equal member. Over the course of time, this attitude is embedded in an athlete's outlook on life. Once accepted, it is understood that what happens in that room, stays in that room. This is where the locker room mentality goes from one generation to the next. It is at the core of the belief system that drives being part of the team. The original purpose of the sport that was introduced to the young player becomes misconstrued. Elements of supremacy are established with the lessons from the sport being transferred to other actions in a player's life. The player becomes conditioned by his sport to use certain words or actions on the field, and then transfer those words or actions into school, often inappropriately hurting other students off the field. Players are told how special and important they are to their school. They believe what is shared without the ability to fully grasp the true meaning of those expectations. They behave in a vacuum, using sport as their standard.

STATISTICALLY SPEAKING...

Research clearly indicates that bullying is a learned behavior and detrimental to the academic, physical, social, and emotional development of all involved—bullies, targets, and the bystanders who witness it. A wave of recent bullying incidents with tragic outcomes has shed a renewed light on this issue. The advent of technology allowing for impulsive, anonymous, and rapid communication has expanded the opportunities for bullying to a degree that necessitates more innovative and immediate responses than ever before.[1]

Parents play right into this mindset as well. Players are told how amazing their talent is by coaches who operate elite programs. Evaluations are performed to further emphasize their future talent. Assumptions are made about a young player's own talent accompanied by dreams about becoming a professional athlete. Parents consider this news to be a chance for the future. Strategies are developed, coaches are hired, and money is spent to create this opportunity. An obsession is shaped around sports—often providing young athletes with the wrong ideas about commitment, achievement, and happiness. Eventually, the formal training process ends. Young players no longer need the direction of their parents to enforce their beliefs. They now have a clear understanding of certain attitudes. The locker room mentality is complete.

There are three customary motives that encourage this locker room mentality: the need for power; causing harm toward others; and receiving recognition. Those involved with sports perceive these motives as being appropriate principles by which to live. They are the three essential characteristics required to be successful in sports. They are also qualities promoted by coaches, shared by players, and defended by parents. However, to outsiders, they are the same traits that identify bullies in the real world. These traits represent behavior that is acceptable on the field, but is questionable off the field. Yet, because of the mindset of sports, the behavior is condoned and allowed to fester.

STRATEGIES AND TACTICS: WHAT BULLIES DO[2]

- Get into frequent fights.
- Put others down.
- Disrespect authority.
- Steal and vandalize property.
- Drink alcohol and smoke.
- Report poor grades.
- Perceive a negative climate.
- Carry a weapon.

ENDNOTES

1 *DuPage County Anti-Bullying Task Force Model Bullying Policy* (2011).
2 Olweus Bullying Prevention Program.

CHAPTER 4

Power

When people see you're happy doing what
you're doing, it sort of takes the power away from
them to tease you about it.
—Wendy Mass, *Every Soul A Star*

Individuals involved with sports usually have a strong drive for power. Because sports require significant physical strength, those who are stronger generally have an advantage. Successful athletes use strength to maximize their force, exploiting a weaker opponent. This supremacy not only includes size, but also the ability to create a perceptional illusion—the mental aspect of sports. Getting into the mind of an opponent requires an understanding of what makes an opponent tick. Often, it comes in the guise of verbal attacks that upset an opponent and force him to lose his focus.

Once this power is harnessed, it can be implemented easily for other uses. The original purpose for which it was attained (winning) gives way to other venues. The power is rarely challenged off the field. The young athlete learns to manipulate this power to his benefit in any situation. Power may take the form of intimidation, trash talking, or creating an environment of helplessness for others.

INTIMIDATION

Self-confidence plays a role in intimidation, whether that confidence is real or fabricated. Some players who intimidate people are overly confident, and they come across as arrogant. Other players actually intimidate because they have low levels of self-confidence. Their actions stem from great insecurities and the need to make themselves feel better. Still other players have natural levels of confidence, but are just plain mean. Regardless of motivation, they all realize that most individuals have common fears—fear of failure, fear of pain, fear of the unknown—and these bullies know how to manipulate those fears. Intimidation feasts on fear. A strong physical presence along with a sharp tongue is common for effective intimidation.

Intimidating an opponent also creates an imbalance of power. Whether through sheer physical force or mental or verbal games, the ability to tip the scales by intimidation is key to success in sports. The teams that can combine the physical and mental elements best are generally the teams doing the victory dance after a game. Intimidating another player can be as simple as a glance or a more sophisticated physical blow.

One of the most common non-physical strategies used by athletes to intimidate others is the use of eye black. Babe Ruth reportedly started the trend by smearing grease under his eyes during afternoon baseball games to reduce the glare. As eye black began to catch on, it spread through baseball and football. Players incorporated smudging the grease under their eyes into their pre-game rituals. It slowly became a regular sports practice and has remained a functional product for years. Those individuals who support this custom say that "eye black" is a ritual in preparation for a game. It is used to motivate players to win the battle and designed to intimidate opponents and create an added edge.

STATISTICALLY SPEAKING...

- Students who participate in bullying are more likely than their peers to vandalize property, to drop out of school, and to use alcohol, cigarettes, or marijuana.[1]
- Boys report that they were most frequently bullied by other boys; it's more common for girls to be bullied by both girls and boys.[2]

Another relatively new, non-physical intimidation tactic is the "Haka." It's a traditional ancestral war cry from the Māori people of New Zealand that consists of a posture dance performed by a group, with vigorous movements, stamping of the feet, and rhythmically shouted accompaniment.[3] To most people, the Haka is a war dance. But in sports, players typically perform the dance prior to a game to get psyched and intimidate their opponents. Players claim the "Haka" is all good-natured fun that further enhances team building. But others claim it is defamatory to a religious custom and unnecessary in youth sports.

> **HAKA**
>
> If you want to watch a typical Haka dance, check it out on YouTube.

There are also a number of ways to intimidate others physically. A person who has a large physical stature is already at an advantage. Size creates a perceptional imbalance that lets a target know he is not able to match his bully's size. Size is not necessarily based on height, but also includes muscle tone and build. Through visual strength, an opponent potentially fears being hurt. Visible anger is also an important contributing factor that enhances the physical element of intimidation. Size combined with emotional instability is a dangerous combination.

Physical intimidation can also be misconstrued as part of the game. For example, it occurs in baseball when a pitcher throws inside to a hitter to brush him off the plate. Or you can find it at a soccer game when a player goes to slide tackle, but ends up taking the feet out from underneath an opponent. Basketball players deliberately foul one another, and the fouls are often overlooked by referees or simply not seen. Football probably exhibits the greatest amount of physical acts toward one another.

Intimidation in sports also masks itself in the form of competition. From an outsider's perspective, it may be difficult to detect, because it can manifest itself under the guise of winning and losing. Phrases such as "it brings out the competitive nature" or "that's just how athletes are wired" are used as justifications. However, intimidation is a main component of bullying behavior. Being able to tip the scales at the expense of another by intimidating them is part of the culture in sports. Unfortunately, an athlete often takes this behavior and applies it to the classroom or the hallways of school. The individual who is on the receiving end of this behavior responds with fear. Whether it is a simple look or words along with an action, the target realizes what is happening and knows immediately that he is facing an unpleasant situation.

Some of the biggest known bullies in schools are involved in athletics. Whether it is the coaches who bring in the booster money receiving preferential treatment, or players who get special recognition in competition, the culture surrounding sports plays out in school as well. Some teams require the players to wear their jerseys on game day, while other teams want their players to dress up wearing khakis, a shirt, and a tie. Those days present opportunities for members of the team to stand out from the rest of the school population. It can be quite intimidating to watch a group of football, basketball, or hockey players walking down the hallway in their jerseys.

TRASH TALKING

Talking trash is the terminology used in sports when nasty comments are directed toward other players. It includes verbal putdowns designed to get "inside" the head of an opponent, thereby creating an edge. Trash talking has been around for centuries; however, trash talking crosses the line when comments are discriminatory in nature. There are many who agree that trash talking is part of the game when done "between the lines"—that is, in the spirit of the game, hopefully yielding an advantage to win. However, when witnessing trash talking on its own, it often comes across as a form of bullying, as it is meant to foster an imbalance of power from one player or team to another.

People who watch sports on TV when a player is "mic'd up" often hear firsthand the comments that are exchanged during the game. Proponents say it's acceptable because it helps the player get an edge to get "inside" the head of his opponent and exploit the mental aspect of the game. Opponents, on the other hand, say that the hurtful comments are meant to degrade the other person, and argue it is simply bullying in disguise—two very different viewpoints.

CLEVER TRASH TALKING

One of the greatest trash talkers of all time was Muhammad Ali, born Cassius Marcellus Clay Jr. In the 1960s and 1970s, he was the heavyweight-boxing champion of the world. Ali was an incredible athlete and genuinely admired and renowned throughout the world. He used his popularity to address political issues, while adhering to a core set of values. However, what separated him from so many others were his cleverly timed comments. He brought trash talking to an entirely innovative and new level. He had an uncanny way of using words as a form of hyperbole and entertainment. His comments were funny, poetic, and got his opponents riled up. However, they were funny more than hurtful.

Here are a few of the more popular quotes:

"This guy is done. I'll stop him in one."

"I float like a butterfly, and I sting like a bee."

"I'll beat him so hard he'll need a shoehorn to put his hat on!"

"He's so ugly that when he cries, the tears run down the back of his head!"

"I've seen George Foreman shadow boxing, and the shadow won!"

Ali was a master of this strategy and always able to garner support from the fans while delivering his message to the intended target.

Unfortunately, trash talking eventually makes its way out of sports and into other relationships and conversations. This type of verbal exchange was meant for a competitive environment, but it is easily adaptable to everyday remarks. There is a very fine line between comments that are meant in jest and insults that are designed to inflict damage.

Anyone with a sharp tongue can utilize it to hurt others. Talking trash is often the root cause that creates fights between races or conflicts between genders. Putting down others becomes a skill that can be honed on the athletic field and played out in the classroom. When comments are shared in the form of trash talk, individuals witnessing the trash talk often use the excuse that the behavior is "just having fun" or "just kidding," as if there were no malicious intent. As trash talking usually focuses on relevant traits like race, gender, and sexual orientation, it makes sense that those involved with the exchange can get mixed messages over the perception of the exchange. What makes trash talking relevant is that there are often "truths" hidden within the meaning, which makes it even more hurtful. However, once the line is crossed, it is very important to acknowledge what transpired and get it stopped.

An effective trash talker makes comments that are personal. He has an uncanny ability to be creative, zeroing in on specific traits. He is relentless in doing whatever he can to get "inside the head" of the other person. As he builds himself up, he simultaneously puts his opponent down. He often creates a small audience as he attacks the other person. It becomes a contest of wits with the cleverest one standing in the end. He will poke fun at weight, appearance, and skills—anything that offers him a psychological advantage. In some situations, he will make harmful comments about a person's family and loved ones. In the end, the adage "Sticks and stones will break my bones, but words will never hurt me" will not work. These comments are meant to be hurtful, but humorous enough to be passed off as harmless teasing.

HELPLESSNESS

The silent component of the locker-room mentality is the feeling of help-lessness that it creates, which is detrimental to both the players and team. A negative culture occurs over time, and the players, coaches, and parents simply choose to turn a "blind eye" to the offensive behavior or condone it. A player may want to speak with the coach about his playing time; however, there is a negative perception that talking to the coach will make matters worse. Instead of speaking about the concern, the player feels helpless and does nothing. But he does share his frustration with his parents. They become concerned and want to speak with the coach directly. The player begs them not to do anything, thus creating a helpless environment for the parents as well.

LEARNED HELPLESSNESS

Parents

Martin Seligman's foundational experiences and theory of Learned Helplessness offer an ideal insight into why this occurs. When people feel they have no control over a situation, they become helpless and no longer look for opportunities for relief or change. When a bully culture exists, it is passed on as acceptable behavior. Those who are part of the bully culture are not even aware of its existence. Some acknowledge its presence, but feel helpless to do something about it. Learned Helplessness does not necessarily occur in all aspects of someone's life. A parent may be able to advocate for himself at work and stand up for what is right. But that same parent may recognize something occurring on his child's team and feel helpless to confront it.

"That's So Gay"

Another example is the use of the word "gay." By the time athletes reach high school, it is likely they have been taught that the word "gay" is derogatory and unacceptable. They know which words are inappropriate, but in sports, homophobia is so pervasive that when they hear someone call a teammate gay or a fag, they do nothing about it. They know it's wrong, but feel helpless to do anything about it. There are many reasons why a player chooses not to confront this behavior. It's possible they think the behavior will turn on them. They don't want to be seen as weak, or simply do not possess the necessary skills to stand up and do the right thing. Nonetheless, the sense of helplessness is so overwhelming they condone the behavior in an attempt to fit in.

Hazing

Most players also realize there is a sacred bond among teammates. Many teams have various traditions that have been passed on year after year. If a certain ritual occurs that is used to initiate young players, they will abide by the unwritten rules—whether it is the freshman who carries equipment or a new player standing up in front of the team singing a song, players are aware of their intended role in these customs. They would rather be part of the team than to be seen as a tattletale. Players may realize the inappropriateness of the behavior, but feel helpless in doing anything to stop it. They become unwilling participants at the pleasure of their teammates.

BULLYING IN THE NFL

Bullying appears to be a central component within the Miami Dolphins organization. As evidenced by events in 2013, it appears as if Jonathan Martin was likely in a position of helplessness—that is, he could not find an alternative to what was occurring with a fellow teammate. It may seem peculiar that a professional athlete weighing over 300 pounds appears helpless, but it is likely that is what occurred.

Being helpless does not have anything to do with race, ethnicity, gender, or age. The power of the locker-room mentality is so consuming that a professional football player was paralyzed and unable to deal with the bullying situation. This mentality is so strong that the "manliness" of his abilities were in question, as was his mental fortitude as an athlete. Despite his past performance at Stanford University, the situation became so overwhelming that the only option to stop the harassment was to leave his job. He had to weigh the bullying that he was experiencing against his role as a football player—he chose to leave the team. It demonstrates that size and physical strength have very little to do with a hierarchy of power in which someone is at a disadvantage. Anyone can be helpless.

ENDNOTES

1 *Bullying in U.S. Schools: 2012 Status Report*, "Olweus Bullying Questionnaire," (Hazelden Foundation, 2013).

2 Ibid.

3 http://en.wikipedia.org/wiki/Haka

CHAPTER 5

Causing Harm

It's not the size of the dog in the fight,
but the size of the fight in the dog!
—Archie Griffin, Former NFL Player and Two-Time
Heisman Trophy Winner

The video starts out with a blurred scene from inside a high school locker room. Players are grouped together when a team leader starts to yell.

> RIGHT! Nigga, let's not hold back! We can win this shit!
> Let's show the coaches we can win this shit! Tell those coaches
> they don't know nuttin'!

Video cuts out to the team on the field, kneeling down with each member holding hands as the head coach leads the group in prayer. Players' eyes are closed as they listen to the prayer for a safe and solid win.

The video cuts to game time with the head coach intensely talking with a tight group of players from the offense.

> Get that fucking, mother fucking outside linebacker. When the
> tackle is going through the B-gap, (looking at a player), right? And
> you got that guy, cheat in a little bit, and fuck his shit up. He's right
> there, just ear-hole 'em. You have to come flat and ear-hole him.

Video cuts to a player running off the field in excitement where he is greeted by coaches and players giving one another high-fives.

> You gotta get that fuckin' ball back. Get that fuckin' ball back, baby.

Video cuts to an assistant coach standing on the sideline screaming at the face of a player.

> You gotta be backin' up the tailback. You got it? You can't be
> getting off the edge. Now get your butt out there. I told you to go in.
> Get the f'ck in the game.

Videos just like this can be viewed anytime on YouTube. A simple search for bullying in sports yields plenty of videos that anyone can watch. This scene plays itself out on fields throughout the country daily with coaches cursing at players to motivate them to win. Some coaches acknowledge the most physical plays of the game by offering game balls and stickers to promote others to join in future rough physical hits. Players are encouraged to do whatever is necessary physically to win. If it involves the possibility of injuring someone else, it is just part of the game. When the other team's star player gets hurt, an advantage is immediately created. Coaches then change their game plan to attack the weak point, doing as much damage as possible to ensure a victory.

The focus on sports-related injuries has increased ten-fold over the past few decades. It is no accident that concussions are now at the forefront of the news. Only a few years ago an athlete would bang his head and come out of the game to be checked. The coach would ask the player how he felt, wondering whether or not he could return to the game. The answer was almost always "yes," so the player was able to return. There were no signs of significant trauma. Players wanted to play, and coaches wanted their players to play. Now there are strict protocols in place to ensure that a player with a concussion is taken out of the game. Coaches can no longer put players' lives at risk. Research now demonstrates just how serious concussions can be and the long-term consequences to head injuries.

Coaches promote the importance of overpowering opponents at the expense of injuring others. Players push themselves in order to compete at the highest level to win championships. Parents turn a blind-eye because of the possibility of a scholarship to college. The window for college opportunities is small. Whether a player has the ability to play D1 or D3, there are only four years to play in high school, and each one matters. Missing a year because of an injury is unacceptable. So players do whatever they can to compete, and playing when hurt is common.

The mindset and acts of aggression that promote injuries translates into the stereotypical bully. The yelling, pushing, and forceful behavior become part of an athlete's routine. For some, it is hard to leave that behavior on the field and not have it cross over to the schoolyard and real life. The physical desire to cause harm to a weaker person is part of being an athlete. It allows the mean-spirited individual to take advantage of other people through embarrassing remarks or destructive acts. Injuring someone is simply a means to an end. Hurtful comments are directed at a target, creating injuries from the inside out.

ARE PLAYERS PUSHED TOO MUCH?

It is a fact that medical professionals have seen an increase in sports-related injuries in the past 10 years. Whether it's concussions, torn ACLs, or Tommy John surgeries, research has shown a dramatic increase in these procedures. The American Orthopedic Society for Sports Medicine (AOSSM) held its annual meeting in Baltimore, MD in July 2012. One of the featured topics that drew a lot of discussion was the S.T.O.P. program (Sports Trauma and Over-Use Prevention). STOP is a well-intentioned awareness effort directed primarily at educating the parents of children who participate in sports about injury reduction and other ways to minimize the risks associated with sports-related activities.[1]

STATISTICALLY SPEAKING...

- Approximately 8,000 children are treated in emergency rooms each day for sports-related injuries.[2]

- High school athletes suffer 2 million injuries, 500,000 doctor visits, and 30,000 hospitalizations each year.[3]

- A history of injury is often a risk factor for future injuries, making prevention critical.[4]

- 62 percent of organized sports-related injuries occur during practices.[5]

- 400,000 brain injuries (concussions) occurred in high school athletics during the 2008-09 school year.[6]

- Concussion rates more than doubled among students age 8-19 participating in sports like basketball, soccer, and football between 1997 and 2007, even as participation in those sports declined.[7]

- High school athletes who have been concussed are three times more likely to suffer another concussion in the same season.[8]

In addition to the physical concerns, there are also the psychosocial challenges that are placed on athletes when playing sports. Regardless of where it comes from, pushing players to win can have detrimental consequences. Some argue that pushing athletes helps create a strong work ethic. It facilitates life-long skills necessary to persevere through challenges, and also establishes a level of excellence that lays the foundation for a successful life. Others contend that the potential for drastic psychological bad effects outweighs the positive. The stressors from competitive sports can induce depression, low self-esteem, and eventually cause the player to leave the sport altogether.

The culture of pushing athletes can have drastic backlashes—it allows bullying behavior to exist, whether it is recognized or not. For example, kids watch how their role models behave on the sports field, and then they act in similar ways elsewhere. They emulate their heroes by taking on the behaviors of those they observe. A coach may push her players to achieve their best, yet players often interpret that behavior as "win at all costs," which means that losing is unacceptable.

HOMOPHOBIA

There is a provocative target in sports that always draws attention. Individuals who identify themselves as LGBT (Lesbian, Gay, Bisexual or Transgender) are constant targets of athletes. A significant amount of harm is directed toward them because they do not conform to the stereotypes of traditional beliefs. When a young individual does not fall within the expected sports typecast, he becomes a target of humor, ridicule, and embarrassment. Homophobia is extremely ingrained in sports. It occurs in gym class, as well as organized athletics. It is the proverbial "white elephant" in the room. Everyone involved knows it exists and witnesses its presence. However, very few have the courage to help create the necessary changes. People in the field have documented research and the requisite skills to address it, but most coaches and parents choose to ignore it and hope it goes away.

STATISTICALLY SPEAKING...

Many LGBT students are harassed or assaulted while playing on sports teams or attending P.E. classes. More than half of LGBT students are bullied or harassed in their P.E. class because of their sexual orientation or gender expression, and over a quarter of them report being harassed or assaulted while playing on a school sports team.[9]

33% of all students who say bullying behavior occurs at school say that it's because the target is not good at sports.[10]

LGBT high school students are about half as likely to play interscholastic sports as their peers.[11]

Biased remarks at school:[12]

- 84.9% of students heard "gay" used in a negative way (for example, "that's so gay") frequently or often at school, and 91.4% reported that they felt distressed because of this language.

- 71.3% heard other homophobic remarks (e.g., "dyke" or "faggot") frequently or often.

- 61.4% heard negative remarks about gender expression (not acting "masculine enough" or "feminine enough") frequently or often.

- 56.9% of students reported hearing homophobic remarks from their teachers or other school staff; and

- Remarks about students not acting "masculine enough" were more common than remarks about students not acting "feminine enough."

The attitudes that are fostered through sports often begin at the moment of birth. Once the hospital chooses the hat or blanket for the newborn (some hospitals have multi-colored items), the family begins to follow the expected gender identification of their child. For a boy, the father is expected to promote sports. For girls, the mother may want the father to quell his desire to push sports, as it may eventually cause an identity problem and have his daughter referred to as a "tomboy." Although stereotypes are changing in our society and in sports, there are still some common misconceptions and gender beliefs that males are better athletes than females. There is also a certain norm regarding the look and actions of an athlete. A male athlete is supposed to be muscular and tough. He has to be able to carry out the masculine attitude toward life, thereby impacting all of his relationships. A female athlete also is supposed to be a certain type. Women in sports are often referred to (inappropriately) as "butch" or "dyke" because of their athletic stature. Young players with homophobic beliefs can exacerbate this mindset. They are unwilling to accept individuals who do not fulfill this stereotypical role.

AN ATHLETE'S STORY—BILLIE JEAN KING

Billie Jean King, born Billie Jean Moffitt, was born November 22, 1943. She began playing tennis at an early age, quickly becoming one of the best players in the world. Between 1961-1979 she won a record 20 Wimbledon titles, 12 U.S. titles, four French titles, and two Australian titles. She was equally successful off the court fighting for equal prize money for men and women. She attained notoriety for her 1973 "Battle of the Sexes" match against Bobby Riggs, who claimed the women's game of tennis to be inferior to men's. King bested Riggs 6-4, 6-3, 6-3 in front of a worldwide television audience of nearly 50 million people. Although she was married for over 20 years, she become one of the first prominent American athletes to openly admit to having a gay relationship. One of her most famous quotes was, "A champion is afraid of losing. Everyone else is afraid of winning."

This homophobic culture is highly visible and extremely toxic in sports. Words like "gay," "fag," or "lesbo" are slung around on a regular basis, and are intended to be hurtful and demeaning. There is a complete lack of acceptance for diversity of any kind in the world of sports. There are numerous stories of professionals who are gay, but in the confines of the locker room, those same players make a conscious decision to remain silent. If they did decide to be truthful to their teammates, it is very likely they would be exiled with the possibility of physical harm.

AN ATHLETE'S STORY—GLENN BURKE

In November 2010, movie producers Sean Maddison and Doug Harris premiered their documentary *Out: The Glenn Burke Story*. It is a difficult story to hear, not only because it occurred in our recent past, but also because of the way it ends. Burke was a natural athlete who excelled in two sports, basketball and baseball, and received professional offers for both. He chose baseball and quickly worked his way up from the minors to the Major League, where he landed a spot on the Los Angeles Dodgers as an outfielder and started Game One of the 1977 World Series.

Burke was funny with a remarkable outgoing personality. According to the documentary, he invented one of the most popular gestures in all of sports: the "high five."[13] Early in his career, Burke felt he had to hide his true nature from his teammates. However, Burke was outspoken, and it became obvious to his teammates that he was gay. Burke was not necessarily "out," but he did unconventional things that drew attention in the locker room. And mostly he refused to lie. When he began to reveal glimpses into his sexuality, the baseball establishment began to shut him out. The issue then became one of guilt-by-association: "If Burke is gay, what does that say about his teammates and baseball in general?"[14]

As bad as the players were, management was much worse. Burke was told outright that he needed to get married to a woman. His response? Not only did he refuse to marry a woman, but he started dating the estranged gay son of famed Dodgers manager Tommy Lasorda. Lasorda responded by trading Burke off to a losing team in Oakland.

Gay rumors followed Burke to Oakland, and he found himself subjected to yet another blatantly homophobic manager, Billy Martin. Burke's career trajectory went downhill even faster from there. He walked away from the game he loved in 1980.

Soon out of the professional game entirely, Burke turned to gay leagues where he became a celebrity in the Castro district of San Francisco. In 1982, he officially came out in an article in *Inside Sports* and on *The Today Show* with Bryant Gumbel. However, his income started to diminish, and he developed a growing drug and alcohol problem. He eventually ran into financial troubles. He turned to theft and was sent to prison. In the end, he died of HIV/AIDS-related causes in 1995.

Since Glenn Burke, nearly 7,000 baseball players have come and gone. Although the numbers of professional athletes who have come out have increased, those that do often face unwelcome scrutiny. Critics offer their personal opinions, forcing these athletes to survive in isolation. The homophobic culture that exists in sports still requires a remarkable individual with incredible character to openly be the person he is, both inside and outside.

The issue of gay players in sports reared its ugly head once again during media day at Super Bowl LXVII in New Orleans in February 2013. Chris Culliver, the San Francisco 49ers cornerback, openly discussed his thoughts on the possibility of having gay teammates with a well-known radio personality. The second-year veteran made it clear in the interview that he would not accept a gay teammate.

"I don't do the gay guys. I don't do that," Culliver said, when asked if a homosexual player ever had approached him. He also indicated that a gay player would not be welcome on the 49ers when asked if there were any gay players on the team. "We ain't got no gay people on the team," Culliver said and continued, "They gotta get up out here if they do. Can't be with that sweet stuff. ... Nah, can't be ... in the locker room, man."

When asked if a gay player should keep his sexual orientation a secret, Culliver stated that gay players should reveal their sexuality after retiring. "Gotta come out 10 years after that," Culliver said.

Shortly after the story ran with his comments, the NFL, 49ers, and Culliver quickly did what they could to correct the situation. In a follow-up statement issued by Culliver, he stated, "The derogatory comments I made yesterday were a reflection of thoughts in my head, but they are not how I feel. It has taken me seeing them in print to realize that they are hurtful and ugly. Those discriminating feelings are truly not in my heart. Further, I apologize to those who I have hurt and offended, and I pledge to learn and grow from this experience."

Unfortunately, regardless of his follow-up statement, his sentiments and remarks are more the norm than not. They are ugly, unacceptable, and must no longer be allowed to be a part of our vernacular anywhere within our American society. How can we tell our young athletes to accept others and refrain from inappropriate comments and actions when their role models on the field do otherwise?

HAZING

There are subtle differences and nuances between bullying behavior and hazing, but if we refer back to the initial components of bullying (aggression, repetition, and an imbalance of power), there is a strong correlation between the two. The difference is that the repetition in hazing eventually has an end, whereas bullying has no end in sight. There are frequent misconceptions about hazing, including the idea that hazing is nothing more than harmless pranks. The reality is that hazing activities occur in many different arenas, take place in both men's and women's organizations, and are common among student groups in middle/high schools and particularly athletic teams.[15]

THE RISKS OF HAZING

In March 2008, Dr. Elizabeth J. Allan and Dr. Mary Madden from the University of Maine, presented "Hazing in View: College Students at Risk."[16] Although one of the main purposes of the study was to focus on hazing in colleges, they discovered a number of key findings that directly relate to high school athletes. The study found that 47% of students in college were hazed while in high school. The hazing occurred in a range of co-curricular high school activities including athletics, ROTC, performing arts, band, and other school activities.[17] Hazing behaviors in high school were assorted in nature but included illegal activities.

The most frequently reported statistics were the following: 28% were told to associate with specific people and not others; 21% were told to sing or chant by themselves or with a selected group; 10% experienced being yelled,

screamed, or cursed at by other members of the group; 12% had to participate in a drinking game; 12% were deprived of sleep; 12% were required
to get a tattoo or body piercing; 11% drank large amounts of non-alcoholic
beverages; 11% had to endure harsh weather conditions without proper
clothing; 9% were awakened by other members during the night; 8% were
forced to make prank telephone calls or harass others; and 8% drank
alcoholic beverages until the point of getting sick or passing out.[18]

Another interesting discovery found that a gap existed between student
experiences of hazing and their recognition of specific behaviors as hazing or
their willingness to label it as such. Eight out of ten individuals who reported
experiencing a specific hazing behavior while in high school did not consider
her/himself to have been hazed.[19] And, most unexpectedly, much hazing
appeared to occur in view of adults, both in school and in the community.[20]
Much of the reported hazing in high schools occurred during initiations
related to athletic teams with many problems arising during pre-season sports
camps. Some of the high profile hazing incidents in the news have involved
brutal initiations in high school sports.[21]

STATISTICALLY SPEAKING...

National Study of College Student Hazing reported the following:[22]

- 55% of college students involved in clubs, teams, and organizations
  experience hazing.

- Hazing occurs in, but extends beyond, varsity athletics and Greek-letter
  organizations and includes behaviors that are abusive, dangerous, and
  potentially illegal.

- Alcohol consumption, humiliation, isolation, sleep-deprivation, and sex
  acts are hazing practices common across types of student groups.

- There are public aspects to student hazing: 25% of coaches or organization advisors were aware of the group's hazing behaviors; 25% of the
  behaviors occurred on campus in a public space; in 25% of the hazing
  experiences, alumni were present.

- In more than half of the hazing incidents, a member of the offending
  group posts pictures on a public web space.

- More students perceive positive rather than negative outcomes of hazing.

- In 95% of the cases where students identified their experience as
  hazing, they did not report the events to campus officials.

- Students recognize hazing as part of the campus culture.

- 69% of students who belonged to a student activity reported they were aware of hazing activities occurring in student organizations other than their own.

- Students report limited exposure to hazing prevention efforts that extend beyond a "hazing is not tolerated" approach.

- 47% of students come to college having experienced hazing.

- Nine out of ten students who have experienced hazing behavior in college do not consider themselves to have been hazed.

Hazing at the high school level is particularly troubling because the developmental stages of adolescence create a situation in which many students are more vulnerable to peer pressure due to the tremendous need to belong, make friends, and find approval in their peer groups. Further, the danger of hazing at the high school level is heightened by the lack of awareness and policy development/enforcement around this issue. While many colleges and universities in the U.S. have instituted anti-hazing policies and educational awareness programs related to hazing, very few secondary schools have done the same.[23] Hazing practices in high schools are often overlooked and dismissed as mere "traditions" because students, parents, teachers, coaches, and administrators do not understand the definition of hazing and how it operates in society.

RITE OF PASSAGE?

The "Slut List" September 2009

The principal of a top-ranked New Jersey high school says it has gone on for a decade: Annual hazing by senior girls who create a "slut list" of incoming freshmen for the first day of school.

"Every year these senior girls—there is usually that one clique, I don't know what you'd call it, a group of girls who create a so-called slut list of incoming freshman girls," said a recent graduate. "It basically consists of a list of girls and little blurbs of something degrading."

A dozen or more names are written on a piece of notebook paper, with crass descriptions, and copies are passed around—hundreds this year, some say. "We've had girls—which is one of the bad things—obsessed that their names are on it, and girls who were upset that they didn't make the list," said the principal. "It's basically vulgar." For about 10 to 15 years now, popular senior girls have developed the list and passed it around, according to former classmates. "This year it was created at an alcohol-fueled party, and it was worse than ever," said one current senior.

A couple of the comments were, "I'm so desperate and horny that I'll give you [drugs] for free if you get with me" and "Keeping up with the family tradition, [blank] me ... and knock me up." The list is just part of what happens on the first day of school, students say. Seniors also blow loud whistles at freshmen, shove them into lockers, and, in years past, slapped stickers on their backs labeling the girls "sluts" or "whores."

Although many parents have complained about the list, about a dozen current and former students said the whole thing is being blown out of proportion. Some girls even want the attention of being on this list and feel left out if they're not on it, said some students. The girls who are on the list, they said, are the very same popular girls who, as seniors, haze the newcomers. And according to a freshman, the first day's hazing is not as bad as many believe, and is all in good fun. "I think they're taking stuff and twisting it ... really it's all fun. It wasn't anything bad."

One of the seniors wrote a Facebook message saying, "The list is just a silly tradition that is cyclical. It won't stop because seniors feel the need to initiate the incoming freshman. For all the parents who are complaining about the list, you have to wonder what they're going to do when their daughters are seniors making it."*

* Christopher Dela Cruz, "Hazing, bullying is increasing concern at Millburn High School," *New Jersey Star Ledger*, (September 18, 2009).

Many who are aware of hazing activities do not concern themselves with confronting the behavior because of the popular myths and misconceptions that are attached to the term. Hazing is not about harmless traditions or silly antics. Hazing is about the abuse of power and the violation of human dignity.[24] In addition, hazing is ingrained into a person's psyche to relative degrees because it is often done secretly, which creates a challenging problem to address. It takes a unique and courageous individual to stand up against hazing for it to be truly changed. Ironically, the hazing behavior is inconsistent with the values of the school/organization, the values of good sportsmanship, and the stated values and purposes that the teams and clubs are attempting to promote.

ENDNOTES

1 http://www.stopsportsinjuries.org/.

2 L. Wier, A. Miller, C. Steiner. *Sports injuries in children requiring hospital emergency care, 2006,* Agency for Healthcare Research and Quality, Rockville, MD (2009). *HCUP Statistical Brief,* No. 75. http://www.hcup-us.ahrq.gov/reports/statbriefs/sb75.pdf.

3 Centers for Disease Control and Prevention. *Sports-related injuries among high school athletes, United States, 2005-06 school year.* MMWR Morbid Mortal Weekly Report. 2006 55(38), 1037-1040. http://www.cdc. gov/mmwr/preview/mmwrhtml/mm5538a1.htm.

4 K.L. Kucera, S.W. Marshall, D.T. Kirkendall, P.M. Marchak, W.E. Garrett, Jr., "Injury history as a risk factor for incident injury in youth soccer." *British Journal of Sports Medicine,* 39(7), (2005), 462.

5 Ibid.

6 E. Yard, R. Comstock, "Compliance with return to play guidelines following concussion in U.S. high school athletes, 2005-2008," *Informa Healthcare,* 23(11), (2009), 888-898.

7 L. Bakhos, G. Lockhart, R. Myers. "Emergency department visits for concussion in young child athletes," *Pediatrics,* 126(3), (2010), e550-e556.

8 L.M. Gessel, S.K. Fields, C.L. Collins, R.W. Dick, R.D. Comstock, "Concussions among United States high school and collegiate athletes," *Journal of Athletic Training,* 42(4), (2007), 495-503.

9 *2011 GLSEN National School Climate Survey Full Report,* pg 52.

10 GLSEN and Harris Interactive, *Playgrounds and Prejudice: Elementary School Climate in the United States, A Survey of Students and Teachers.* New York: GLSEN, (2012).

11 Joseph G. Kosciw, Ph.D., Emily A. Greytak, Ph.D., Mark J. Bartkiewicz, M.S., Madelyn J. Boesen, M.A., Neal A. Palmer, M.S. *The 2011 National School Climate Survey: The experiences of lesbian, gay, bisexual and transgender youth in our nation's schools.* New York: GLSEN, (2012), pg 52.

12 *2011 GLSEN National School Climate Survey Full Report,* pg. xiv.

13 *Out: The Glenn Burke Story.* Documentary film produced by Doug Harris and Sean Maddison, 2010.

14 Ibid.

15 http://www.stophazing.org/high_school_hazing/index.htm

16 Elizabeth J. Allan, Ph.D. and Mary Madden, Ph.D., *Hazing in View: College Students at Risk, Initial Findings from the National Study of Hazing*, (2008).

17 Ibid.

18 Ibid.

19 Ibid.

20 Ibid.

21 Nadine C. Hoover, Ph.D., Norman J. Pollard, EdD, *Study by Alfred University and the NCAA*, 1999

22 University of Maine, *Hazing in View: College Students at Risk*, (2008) Executive Summary.

23 Ibid.

24 Ibid.

CHAPTER 6

Rewards

If winning isn't everything, why do they keep score?
—Vince Lombardi, Football Legend

The Lombardi Trophy, Stanley Cup, Commissioner's Trophy, an Olympic gold medal, the Green Jacket—these desirable awards represent a small sampling of the most coveted honors in sports. They are the dreams of athletes and one of the reasons they choose to compete. But only a fortunate few ever have the opportunity to grasp one of these trophies in victory, legitimately calling it their own. Those athletes instantly become the envy of others who have wanted to hold one, but failed. They are the guidepost of excellence that signifies all of the good that sports symbolize.

THE POSITIVE ASPECTS

These rewards create one of the greatest components of sports. They offer the player a plan toward excellence. From the professional to the recreational player, these awards represent the opportunity to achieve greatness—by being the best in that moment in time. They are the symbol and recognition of hard work, commitment, and perseverance. They are memories that last a lifetime. Regardless of an athlete's age, anyone who is in a position to win that first-place trophy celebrates as if it is a national championship. The effort needed is no less significant to that athlete than those who are at the professional level. The winning athlete becomes the focus of every talk a coach makes to her team in the locker room. The players rally around the cause of winning the trophy, while the parents promote its significance as it creates additional opportunities to showcase their players' skills.

Sports also offer a number of other rewards for individuals. The physical component of athletics encourages a healthy life style. A young player learns the value of exercise and conditioning through sports, creating habits that last throughout life. Whether it's aerobic or weight conditioning, the training that is encouraged in sports gives athletes the opportunity to develop appropriate habits.

The mental aspects of sports give athletes the opportunity to learn much needed lessons that can be translated into other aspects of life. The will to win and overcome adversity are valuable lessons that are essential in other parts of life, including academics, careers, and relationships. The education learned through sports is difficult to duplicate in an academic arena, so it can be an essential component of learning about life's challenges.

The social rewards are also very significant. Popularity comes with being a good athlete. It is easier to gain friends through sports than any other arena. It can become a common denominator between two strangers on a bus who immediately connect over a recent sports event without ever having another thing in common. Sports are what draw people together socially, joining them in a universal story. The ability to connect immediately around sports makes the initial bonding easier. The friendships that are made through sports seem to last longer and have greater meaning than other relationships. The memories that are created in sports transcend all other life experiences that can be carried into adulthood.

Corporate leaders look for those individuals with a background in sports. The skills that athletes possess are an ideal match to the traits needed to be successful in the workforce. Athletes understand the power of teamwork, have a work ethic that matches, and are willing to sacrifice their personal goals for the betterment of the team.

THE NEGATIVE ASPECTS

However, there is a flip side. Underneath all of the greatness that sports offer lies an undercurrent of dishonesty, which involves greed, performance-enhancing drugs, questionable moral behavior, entitlement, and preferential treatment based on a distinct level of customized standards. This aspect of sports is swept under the rug and rears its ugly head only when something goes astray in the news. It is the proverbial "white elephant" that everyone knows exists, yet few choose to address. The locker room culture justifies this deceit and allows it to continue.

Greed creates numerous unreasonable expectations in sports. Coaches constantly focus on perfection and are never satisfied with their number of wins or championships. They constantly chase their next victory with the goal of creating a grand sports dynasty. In their quest for greatness, coaches use bully tactics to get the most out of their players. The end justifies the means because their coaching style provides wins. Over time, their selfish pursuit becomes an excessive desire for more.

Players also have the same hunger as their coaches. Coming from a winning team increases their chance to play at the next level. Student athletes see the amount of money being made by professionals and fantasize about their own chances at fame and fortune. They believe they are better than others and see themselves belonging to an untouchable part of an elite group. This feeds a bully mentality, allowing athletes to assume they are more relevant and valued than others. Their greed transcends all other elements of rational reasoning, creating a toxic environment that is conducive to an imbalance of power. Anyone willing to challenge this balance is quickly reminded of his place in the hierarchical structure.

Parents can easily get caught up in this greed mentality as well. In particular, if they have the financial means, they can pay for elite coaching and personal trainers. Thus, they gain bragging rights to the number of trophies their child has on the living room mantle. The dreams that parents have for their players include glory and recognition. Having their child achieve these goals in sports gives tremendous satisfaction to parents, regardless of the cost. The ability to claim that their athlete plays a college sport or plays for a professional team garners incredible respect and praise. Through association, they, too, have an elite status that is validated through the acceptance of others. In this situation, some parents end up placing undue emphasis on athletics and the need to be successful, at times forcing an athlete who once loved the game to leave it entirely.

This drive for success permeates all levels in sports. Whether it's a coach, player, or parent, the odds are simply not favorable for reaching college and professional status. The reward is no doubt there, but for nearly all it is unattainable.

CHANCES OF GOING PRO (2011)[1]

ESTIMATED PROBABILITY OF COMPETING IN ATHLETICS BEYOND THE HIGH SCHOOL INTERSCHOLASTIC LEVEL

STUDENT ATHLETES	MEN'S BASKETBALL	WOMEN'S BASKETBALL	FOOTBALL	BASEBALL	MEN'S ICE HOCKEY	MEN'S SOCCER
High School Student Athletes	545,844	438,933	1,108,441	471,025	36,912	398,351
High School Senior Student Athletes	155,955	125,409	316,697	134,579	10,546	113,815
NCAA Student Athletes	17,500	15,708	67,887	31,264	3,944	22,573
NCAA Freshman Roster Positions	5,000	4,488	19,396	8,933	1,127	6,449
NCAA Senior Student Athletes	3,889	3,491	15,086	6,948	876	5,016
NCAA Student Athletes Drafted	48	32	255	806	11	49
Percent High School to NCAA	3.2%	3.6%	6.1%	6.6%	10.7%	5.7%
Percent NCAA to Professional	1.2%	0.9%	1.7%	11.6%	1.3%	1.0%
Percent High School to Professional	0.03%	0.03%	0.08%	0.60%	0.10%	0.04%

Note: These percentages are based on estimated data and should be considered approximations of the actual percentages.

STATISTICALLY SPEAKING...

- Three in 10,000, or approximately 0.03%, of high school senior boys playing interscholastic basketball will eventually be drafted by an NBA team.

- About 6%, or less than 1 in 16, of all high school senior boys playing interscholastic football will go on to play football at a NCAA member institution.

- Eight in 10,000, or approximately 0.08%, of high school senior boys playing interscholastic football will eventually be drafted by an NFL team.

- About 3 in 50, or about 6.4%, of high school senior boys interscholastic baseball players will go on to play men's baseball at a NCAA member institution.

- Less than 1 in 300, or approximately 0.32%, of high school senior boys playing interscholastic ice hockey will eventually be drafted by an NHL team.

- Approximately 1 in 1,250, or approximately 0.07%, of high school senior boys playing interscholastic soccer will eventually be drafted by an MLS team.

THE RISE OF DRUGS

Losing is like quicksand. The harder you work at getting out of it, the deeper you sink. Although it is part of the game, losing is not something coaches and players want to experience too often. Rifts are created between the closest of teammates, while judgment becomes impaired when speaking with others. When these streaks come along, coaches will do whatever is necessary to shift the results back to victories. Players realize the consequences that occur when coaches are faced with these decisions. In order to stay in the lineup to keep contributing to the team, their skills and play must continue to be at the highest level. In some situations, players choose to find alternative methods in order to produce the needed results.

Performance Enhancement Drugs (PEDs) are readily available to athletes beginning early in a high school career. Young players hear about professionals who make these choices, and these stories have a direct impact on their own personal decision-making. Kids read articles in muscle magazines with access to various nutritional supplements at the local store. Coaches encourage off-season conditioning with subtle messages to those who want to compete in upcoming seasons. The temptation to take shortcuts to achieve a necessary physical goal is simply too much for some young athletes. The "get strong quick" fix appears too good to pass up for the possibility of college scholarships or professional opportunities. Combined with the expectation of coaches, players are likely to choose PEDs as an option for ultimate results.

Those that choose this route lack the ability to understand the larger picture. They compromise their long-term personal development for a short-term gain. The chemicals that are absorbed into the body create strong reactions physically, as well as emotionally. One of the most common side effects is increased aggression, the focus of which often targets teammates, opponents, officials, and coaches.

DRUGS IN SPORTS[2]

1954: The first use of anabolic steroids was used by the Soviets to enhance athletic performance.

1970: Arnold Schwarzenegger won his first of seven Mr. Olympia titles with the aid of steroids.

1987: NFL introduced the first anti-steroid policy.

1988: A study by the Journal of AMA found that steroids were being used by 6.6% of high school male athletes.

1999: The World Anti-Doping Agency (WADA) was established.

2013: Lance Armstrong ultimately admitted to doping dating back to 1999 and being a bully.

STATISTICALLY SPEAKING[3]...

- 85% of teen athletes are not educated on the side effects of steroids.
- 44% of teen athletes say it is "very easy" or "fairly easy" to obtain steroids.
- 11% of high school males report trying steroids.
- 40% of teenage steroid users say they are influenced by the fact that pros are using drugs.
- 57% of teen users learn about drug use by reading muscle magazines.
- Steroid users are 56% more likely to experience increases in irritability and aggressive behavior.

THE "BENEFITS" OF BEING AN ATHLETE

Preferential treatment also comes with being an athlete. The worship attitude allows these individuals to live within a different set of standards. At an early age, others view these athletes with a sense of envy. In some instances, the exceptional athlete becomes a target because he is significantly better than everyone else. Groupthink takes over, creating an unexpected reversal of power. Jealous teammates look for opportunities to criticize this player. However, in most situations this athlete does receive unique privileges, often getting away with more than the average person.

It *is* a benefit to being good at a sport. Coaches encourage teachers to be more forgiving with student athletes because it will ultimately be of greater value to the school. This sense of entitlement becomes the foundation of their personal behavior. As they grow through their athletic career, expectations are created for it to continue. But what is the ultimate benefit for athletes in sports? The greed that manifests itself from winning only conditions a player for self-fulfillment. It becomes WIFM, *What's In it For Me*? Nothing else matters at that time. If only a minuscule amount of student athletes ever play in college and beyond, what is the purpose of focusing so much energy on winning games? Why are players being pushed to such an extent? How does a high school athlete benefit by winning a sectional or state championship? How about a 13u tournament during the summer in Delaware? Outside of bragging rights, what lessons are being taught through the framework of sports?

Athletes and coaches are greedy for wins. The overzealous attitude only creates further challenges. The components in sports that provide opportunities to succeed are also the same elements that promote negative behavior. It is time to focus on this component of sports. The culture that has been created must be addressed and understood.

ENDNOTES

1 http://www.ncaa.org/wps/wcm/connect/public/ncaa/pdfs/2011/2011+probability+of+going+pro

2 http://www.weighttraining.com/features/steroids-in-sports

3 Ibid.

CHAPTER 7

Who Are the Bullies in Sports?

Repetition is the first lesson in learning.

—Joe Namath, Super Bowl III MVP

The history of organized youth sports in the U.S. can be traced back to the "emergence of boy's work groups as preventive intervention of the social welfare system"[1] in the 1880s. The idea was to provide these youth with leisure activities (sports and other recreational activities) that would keep them out of trouble.

THE RISE OF EXTRACURRICULAR SPORTS

During the 1920s, sports became increasingly popular. Voluntary organizations got involved in providing these kinds of activities. By the late 1930s, this interest increased even more because educators were against providing highly competitive sports for children in schools. Organizations like the YMCA, Boy Scouts, and Boy's Clubs provided supervised recreation. The first Little League Baseball organization began in 1939 as a community project and involved about 200 players. Seventy years later in 2008, Little League had 2.6 million participants in more than 80 countries around the world[2]

Nearly 40 million children and adolescents are involved in youth sports today. They participate in everything from Little League Baseball, Pop Warner Football, and youth hockey leagues to organized swimming, soccer, and cheerleading teams. Parents have invested a lot of money and effort in these activities. U.S. research shows that during the school year, adolescents participate an average of 4-6 hours per week in an organized sport and even more during the summer. In high schools across the country, an average of nearly 60% of the student body participates in at least one sport.

Only the family, school, television, and computer (Internet) have more contact time than sports with children who are participants. This makes sports an important community phenomenon with the potential to impact adolescent development. Sports programs have the capability to enhance positive youth development and serve as a vehicle for prevention interventions.[3]

A "professionalization" of sports has also occurred in the past 20 years. Small businesses offer professional training to the youngest of players. This business approach creates a customer-based philosophy with expected consumer results. Sports are no longer just considered to be recreational activities, but also a competitive approach to create opportunities for possible college scholarships. Not too long ago athletes were able to compete in multiple sports throughout the year. It was common for a player to spend his fall playing football, winter playing basketball, and spring playing baseball. However, today that is simply not the preferred path for parents and players. Coaches are even jumping on this "bandwagon," encouraging players to select one sport early in the formative years.

These professional companies provide coaching to players of all ages. They offer individual skill development, clinics, and camps, as well as the opportunity to compete on independent teams. They promote their services to parents offering the chance to chase dreams of college athletics. It is an expensive luxury that contributes to unreasonable expectations for parents and players. These businesses offer an extremely competitive component that impacts young players early in life. Although many of these programs legitimately care and offer age-appropriate experiences, there are some that seek to solely increase their bottom dollar without regards to the possible negative impact on the child. There is little to no regulation on the businesses that claim to offer appropriate skill sets and physical development training to youths.

THE BULLIES IN SPORTS

Does bullying occur in sports? The answer is an unwavering...yes! Bullying occurs in sports because the culture that exists promotes it. In sports, like life, bullies come in all shapes and sizes. Some bullies are obvious, while others go undetected. The bully is very good at what he does. In many situations, the comments a bully might make are not condemned because the culture condones it. For example, screaming and the use of verbal put-downs are very common in sports. Players call out other players. Coaches degrade players in front of their teams. Parents complain to referees about perceived wrong calls. In any other realm, people would not accept that type of behavior, yet in sports, it is commonplace.

There is no one stereotype of a bully. Although the activities of a bully typically create an imbalance of power, that power may not be manifested solely based on physical strength. All that is really required is for an individual to "perceive" an imbalance of power, thus creating a bully situation. Or there could be a very strong psychological component, which has nothing to do with body size. Anyone can use aggressive behavior toward someone else. There are bullies on the bench, bullies in the coach's box, and bullies in the stands.

BULLY PLAYERS

One thing is certain: Bully Players have an aggressive personality. They are motivated by power with a desire to dominate others. They are likely to be viewed as a leader on the team, yet their approach is negative in nature. They focus on others' perceived deficiencies, putting down teammates when errors are made. They want to maintain their position of power and squash others who are threats to their role. Bully Players also create an imbalance of power with other students within school who are not on a sports team. They see those individuals as lesser people and treat them as such. They also bully others by using inappropriate homophobic slurs.

AN ATHLETE'S STORY—LANCE ARMSTRONG[4]

Lance Armstrong, born Lance Gunderson, is an American former professional cyclist. He is the founder of the Livestrong Foundation that supports cancer patients. He is one of the most famous cyclists in the sport, having won a record seven consecutive Tour de France races between 1999-2005. In 1996, he was diagnosed with testicular cancer that spread to his brain and lungs. However, by February 1997, he was declared cancer-free and resumed his cycling training.

Armstrong was an extremely visible celebrity, promoting his racing and foundation; however, doping allegations constantly followed him throughout his career and retirement. In June 2012, the United States Anti-Doping Agency formerly charged him with the use of illicit performance-enhancing drugs, disqualifying him from his victories in the sport. By August 2012, he was issued a lifetime ban from competition. Despite having denied drug use throughout his career, in January 2013 in a television interview with Oprah Winfrey, Armstrong admitted to doping.

Not only did Armstrong lie and cheat, but he was also a bully. According to sworn witnesses, he "pressured, threatened, and intimidated others." In 2002, he threatened an ex-teammate, Christian Vande Velde, that if he wanted to continue to ride for the Postal Service team he would have to follow Armstrong to "the letter." In 2004, Armstrong threatened cyclist Filippo Simeoni, saying, "You made a mistake when you testified against Ferrari (Armstrong's doctor). I have a lot of time and money, and I can destroy you."

BULLY COACHES

Bully coaches come in different styles. Some are considered "old school," using strict strategies that keep players in line. Some constantly yell, abusing anyone in sight and clearly demonstrating their role as the coach. Some are extremely arrogant, believing that their coaching style is what allows their players to win. Another type of bully coach looks for various loopholes that can be manipulated for a win. Some coaches are a combination of all these characteristics, using the different traits as situations require. Bully coaches have the ability to ruin the fun of the game by losing sight of what truly matters. They get caught up in the emotions of the game by focusing on winning. They are more concerned about their win-loss record than ensuring that their players are enjoying the game.

AN ATHLETE'S STORY—MIKE RICE

Mike Rice, Jr. is a college basketball coach, formerly the head coach at Rutgers University. He gained national attention in April 2013 when ESPN's *Outside The Lines* aired videos from his practices. They showed Rice yelling, pushing, kicking, cursing, using homophobic slurs, and throwing basketballs at players during practices. The videos struck a national nerve, touching off a nationwide outcry and condemning Rice's behavior as a coach. He was quickly fired, with Tim Pernetti, the Athletic Director, following him shortly thereafter.

The videos showed numerous clips of Rice at practice firing basketballs at players and hitting them in the back, legs, feet, and shoulders. He was shown pushing players in the chest, grabbing them by their jerseys, and pulling them around the court. In addition, he could be heard yelling obscenities using gay slurs. The unique twist to this story was that the videos had been shared with the administration in December 2012. An independent investigator had been hired at that time to analyze the tape. Rice was suspended for three games, fined $75,000, and ordered to attend anger management classes. The university president even signed off on the initial punishment.

However, once the story made national headlines, all those involved re-evaluated their decisions, quickly making choices that should have been made at the beginning. Shortly after this incident, Rutgers suspended the men's head lacrosse coach amid accusations of verbal abuse. Furthermore, it appears that Rutgers has a long line of embarrassing incidents with inappropriate basketball coaches. Former head coach Kevin Bannon was fired after a questionable practice decision regarding his players. He ordered two athletes and two managers to run sprints naked during a foul-shooting contest.

BULLY PARENTS

Bully parents are everywhere. They gossip among themselves, challenging every call a coach makes. They aggressively confront coaches about playing time, using their title of "parent" to create an imbalance of power. They stand on the sidelines yelling at officials over calls that go against their team, while cheering on the same referee when calls go in their favor. They live vicariously through their son or daughter by constantly pushing them to get better. They speak arrogantly to other parents, assuming that they have some perceived expertise that is only available to them. Their emotions get the best of them, often interfering with others people's enjoyment of the game. They are blowhards that talk and talk and talk.

AN ATHLETE'S STORY—ANDRE AGASSI

Andre Agassi is an American retired professional tennis player. He is a former ranked No. 1 player in the world, who turned pro in 1986 playing through the mid-2000s. His professional resume includes being an eight-time Grand Slam champion and a 1996 Olympic gold medalist. All throughout his career, he was seen as a role model and leader within the sport. He is the founder of the Andre Agassi Charitable Foundation raising over $60 million for at-risk youth in Southern Nevada. In 2001, he opened the Andre Agassi College Preparatory Academy in Las Vegas, a K-12 public charter school for at-risk youth.

In November 2009, he published an autobiography *Open*, highlighting a number of disturbing insights into his life. Most notably was how he always hated tennis "with a dark and secret passion" because of his overbearing father. He shared that his life in tennis had been chosen by his father. Under his father's hard-nosed tennis instruction, he was drilled not to be beaten. He felt fear if he chose not to play and was often introduced as "The Future #1 Player in the World." His father also gave him a drug called Excedrin before matches because it contained high levels of caffeine.

In 1992, Agassi won his first Grand Slam title at Wimbledon. In a conversation with his father after the victory, his dad commented, "You had no business losing that fourth set." Although it appeared he was living the high life, on the inside, there were major demons. When he was 13, he was sent to the Nick Bollettierri Tennis Camp in Florida to perform at an elite level. However, he learned there how to rebel, smoking marijuana and drinking Jack Daniel's. By his mid-twenties, he was taking the highly addictive stimulant crystal meth to deal with his depression. He tested positive for the illicit drug and tried to cover it up. He was 27 years old when he had an epiphany with his coach, choosing to play tennis for himself.

Identifying the bullies in sports allows us to develop strategies to address these individuals. They have been allowed to go about their way without too many consequences to their behavior. They have existed in the dark, wreaking havoc for generations. However, this negative behavior can no longer go on without accountability. Although awareness around this issue has existed for decades, now is the time to stand up and do something about it.

Over the next few chapters, the three types of bullies in sports will be further discussed with tactics and skills to confront them. In addition, Part III of the book offers a number of strategies for being proactive.

ENDNOTES

1   N. D. Reppucci, "Ecology and prevention: Teenage pregnancy, child sexual abuse, and organized youth sports," *American Journal of Community Psychology,* 15 (1987), p. 13.

2   Institute on Family & Neighborhood Life, Fact Sheet, "Organized Youth Sports: How Do They Affect Children and Adolescents," Clemson University, May 2001.

3   Ibid.

4   http://www.slate.com/articles/newsandpolitics/framegame/2013/01/lancearmstrongsoprahinterviewhisthreatsandbullyingarethereal.html.

CHAPTER 8

The Bully Player

*What if the kid you bullied at school, grew up, and turned
out to be the only surgeon who could save your life?*
—Lynette Mather, Author

Identifying the Bully Player on a sports team is not very difficult. He is easily recognizable; however, the old stereotype of what bullies look like has drastically changed. The physical traits are no longer the sole quality of what a bully looks like, because Bully Players come in all sizes. A Bully Player is very good at what he does. He is often vocal in his opinions, acting as a leader on the team. In some situations, you wouldn't even consider his actions to be bullying behavior. If confronted about his behavior, he may respond that he cares about the team. He wants to win while encouraging everyone to do their best. The Bully Player can be physically strong, often using his strength to intimidate others. He can be impulsively hot-tempered, which arises when things do not go according to his plan. He is fearless in nature, persuading others to follow along. He has high levels of confidence, but lacks empathy for others. He has an uncanny ability to manipulate situations that ultimately end up being beneficial to him.

STATISTICALLY SPEAKING...

- Bullying is the most common form of violence in our society; between 15% and 30% of students are bullies or victims.[1]

- A recent report from the American Medical Association on a study of over 15,000 6th-10th graders estimates that approximately 3.7 million youths engage in, and more than 3.2 million are victims of, moderate or serious bullying each year.[2]

- Direct, physical bullying increases in elementary school, peaks in middle school, and declines in high school. Verbal abuse, on the other hand, remains constant.[3]

- Over two-thirds of students believe that schools respond poorly to bullying, with a high percentage of students believing that adult help is infrequent and ineffective.[4]

- Some studies say that approximately 33% of those who habitually bully will be convicted of a criminal offense in their adult years.

- A longitudinal study in Norway found that 60% of boys identified as "bullies" in middle school had at least one criminal conviction by the age of 24; 35% to 40% had three or more convictions. "Bullies" were three to four times as likely as non-bullying peers to have multiple convictions by their early 20s.[5]

- Students are most often bullied by being called mean names (verbal), having false rumors spread about them (rumors), by being left out on purpose (exclusion), by words or gestures with sexual meaning (sexual), or by being hit, kicked, or pushed (physical)[6]
- 16.2% of students had been electronically bullied, including being bullied through email, chat rooms, instant messaging, websites, or texting, during the 12 months before the survey.[7]

THE BULLY LINE

There are multiple roles that individuals take when it comes to bullying. Some roles are considered aggressive while others are passive. The aggressive roles have a visible impact. The Initiator is the most commonly identified individual. He often begins the negative behavior toward a target. The Motivator adds his own comments while supporting the Initiator. The Cheerleader comes along and focuses his attention on the Motivator and Initiator, thereby encouraging them.

The passive roles have come to the forefront in the past few years. We are now aware just how much these individuals contribute to bullying. The Fanatic observes the situation, enjoying the altercation between the Initiator and the Target. The Spectator stands by simply noticing the acts. The Ostrich puts his "head in the sand" in hopes that the behavior will stop. These bystanders make up the majority of individuals involved, yet do not realize how their involvement, or lack of, negatively impacts this behavior. Their damage is subtle.

The Bully Line offers an innovative description of bullying behavior. It is an educational tool that I created to explain bullying to coaches and athletes. It is a play on "Coach Talk" when plays are designed for game situations. The Bully Line is an important awareness component about bullying that utilizes the mindset of sports. The illustration of the Bully Line, following the explanations, offers a visual example.

- **Initiator:** This person initiates the bullying behavior toward a target and plays a key role as a leader. In sports, this individual is similar to the quarterback in football or a point guard in basketball. He is the leader of the team and considered to be the player on the field who makes the key decisions.

- **Motivator:** This person also engages in the bullying toward the target and takes an active role. He joins the Initiator, making additional comments (actions) toward the target and encouraging the Initiator. In sports, this person walks around with the star athlete or captain. He wears his letter jacket, following the Initiator who is often doing the "dirty work." On the field, this is the athlete who contributes to the win.

- **Cheerleader:** This person is an aggressive bystander. He openly supports what is occurring by laughing and calling attention to what is taking place. He cheers on the Initiator and Motivator by encouraging the bullying behavior. His focus is on those two people. He does not make any additional comments (actions) toward the target. In sports, these bullies are the cheerleaders on the sidelines. They are not directly playing the game, but are extremely involved in motivating the crowd.

- **Fanatic:** This person is a bystander who watches the bullying. He is engaged in the pure entertainment of what is happening. He generally does not have much of an allegiance to either the Initiator/Motivator or the Target. He is just excited to watch what is happening. In sports, this person is similar to the fan who comes to the game dressed up with face paint wearing the team's jersey. He honestly believes his presence at the game has some direct impact on the final result of the game.

- **Spectator:** This person is simply an onlooker. He purposely does not get involved and does not participate in either direction. He might say "it's none of my business" or "glad it's not me." In sports, this person comes to the game, but doesn't really "buy in" to all the hype and over-the-top behavior of the fanatic. He goes because there's nothing really else going on. He doesn't really understand what the big excitement is, but will be there just to have something to do. In bullying, he is glad he is not the Target.

- **Ostrich:** This person is in the majority. He knows it is wrong and dislikes the bullying behavior. He wants to stop it, but feels helpless that there is nothing he can do. He might say, "What can I do?" He knows it is wrong, but does not do anything to stop it He thinks twice about interfering because if he gets involved, the Initiator/Motivator might turn on him. So he puts his head in the sand and chooses to do nothing.

- **Game Changer, the Upstander:** This person represents a very small percentage of the population. Some research has identified that fewer than one percent of the population has the character to actually do something about it. He wants to help the target. He takes action. The most effective tool to stop the behavior is by removing the Target. The Upstander has no concerns over whether or not the Initiator/Motivator will turn on him. He goes into the group walking out with the Target. In some situations the Upstander knows the Initiator/Motivator and is able to confront them directly. He demands that they stop while simultaneously removing the Target.

THE BULLY LINE

Research shows that nearly 85% of students are bystanders, 10% are targets, and 5% are those that bully others. The specific roles individuals take in the Bully Line are not necessarily limited to an obvious set role. A person can start out as a Cheerleader, but then decide to also make comments toward the Target, thereby going into the Motivator role. An Initiator may begin the bullying and then relinquish that role, becoming more of a Cheerleader or Fanatic. An Initiator may begin bullying in one situation and then on another day take a less active role, becoming a Fanatic. The roles are not exclusive. Individuals can take on the various roles, given the set of circumstances.

The Bystander is by far the largest group of individuals involved in the Bully Line. The Cheerleader is the most aggressive, yet remains focused on the two instigators of the bullying behavior. Although they are active participants, their behavior falls in line with a Bystander, standing by watching the actions take place. As we move down the right of the Bully Line, the Bystander behavior becomes more passive—from the Fanatic to the Spectator to the Ostrich. The final two, Spectator and Ostrich, make up the predominance of the Bystanders in bullying.

There are numerous reasons why people choose the Bystander role. The choice to stand by and do nothing may not be a conscious decision, but it is a subliminal decision. This behavior also becomes learned and forms habits early in a person's life. The four most common reasons why people remain Bystanders are because of fear, doubt, focus, and making things worse than they already are. Fear is the primary reason that people remain silent. They are afraid to approach the individuals. They fear the unknown consequences and prefer not to challenge the status quo already established within the culture. They also doubt if they do tell an adult that anything will truly change from that point forward. Research supports that most adults do not handle the reporting of bullying behavior very efficiently, thus confirming that it's not worth standing up for to begin with. They are also concerned that the focus of the Initiator/Motivator will switch to them. They do not want to find themselves on the end of the negative behavior and believe if they do stand up it will then transfer onto them. The final and possibly most compelling reason is that they believe it will make matters worse than they already are. Time and again they have witnessed other people's choice to stand up, and they see the wrath that took place place. The situation was at least bearable prior to standing up, but after it is perceived as not survivable.

Many individuals see themselves as being a Game Changer and want to be an Upstander. Again, research proves otherwise. Less than one-half of 1% of the population is able to stand up against bullying behavior. A Game Changer is someone who drastically alters the outcome of a game. He is able to perform in the "clutch," rising above all doubt and ability. He is seen as a playmaker inspiring other players, as well as those in the stands. His actions on the field have the ability to transform the game, thus creating new expectations of performance from that point forward. Not everyone in sports is a Game Changer.

Nearly all people believe in their ability to stand up to the aggressive bully. Many people do have the right intentions, but most of them do not have the skill set or character to do something about it. Standing up to a bully requires tremendous emotional strength. The Bully Line is designed to raise their awareness about the different bullying roles and encourage them to be a Game Changer by becoming an Upstander.

The most effective deterrent to bullying is adult intervention. Four- to seven-year-olds are pretty good at finding help, and at that age, getting an adult to intervene is acceptable. However, as children get older, they are less inclined to get help from an adult. The element of trust is no longer present. They learn not be a tattletale. They don't believe anything will really change if they do intervene.

TARGETS

The Bully Player targets a number of different individuals. Some of the most common targets are other students who do not play a sport, as typical bullies tease students who are different from them. Bullies also make racial or homophobic slurs toward players (targets) on other teams. They even challenge officials. In addition, the male Bully Player might make inappropriate comments or advances toward females.

THE G.K. (GAY KID)

In the spring of 2008, a high school athlete playing lacrosse was targeted by his teammates and referred to as simply GK. It didn't seem to matter much to him, because he didn't know what was meant by GK. Throughout the season, the comments continued, but the player was able to just deal with the juvenile behavior. He was also a basketball player and learned that the varsity coach worked at a particular summer camp and was "highly encouraged" to attend the camp. Those players that chose to attend the camp were often given a higher priority and consideration the following season. It wasn't required, but the word on the street was that it was essential if there was any desire to play on the varsity team. He signed up and attended the summer program.

Some of the players from lacrosse also played basketball and attended the camp as well. The teasing continued, but by now the player knew that GK meant "Gay Kid." He put up with it, but it started to get old and unwelcome. He'd make comments to them to stop, but the bullying behavior never really went away. Since it was a sleep-away camp, they lived in the same bunk for the entire session. Unbeknownst to him, they were secretly taking pictures to be used at a later time. The camp program ended, he returned home, and waited for the new school year to begin.

As school started, the bullying behavior and teasing started up again, but this time those who had taken the pictures created a website and put his face and pictures in inappropriate situations. They shared the weblink with other students, and in no time everyone in school was visiting the website, making fun of him, and humiliating him to the point of depression. His parents noticed drastic changes in his mood, behavior, and ultimately his grades. Each time they inquired about what might be going on, he simply just said it was "nothing," and given that he was a teenage boy, they chalked it up to typical adolescent angst. When he could no longer keep his emotions to himself and the humiliation and embarrassment that he encountered became too much, he came clean to his parents and explained what had happened during the previous six months.

(In order to complete his high school education, this student had to change schools, and it came at the expense of the home community.)

The Bully Player focuses his behavior on his teammates. He believes that bullying helps motivate other players. He wants to push them harder. He views himself as a team leader for promoting the bullying behavior. He calls out players who make errors or drop the ball. The Bully Player teases players who do not get a lot of playing time and sit on the bench. Often, the Bully Player concentrates on the youngest members of the team and requires them to go through various initiations or traditions that he went through when he joined the team. Athletes who are subjected to bullying often lose focus, feel anxious, or quit sports altogether. In addition, they're reluctant to tell an adult because they are embarrassed or feel shame. The Bully Player can be heard yelling at targets and criticizing their ability. He blames the Target for errors, using repeated put-downs. He makes unreasonable demands, while denying another player's accomplishments. He uses inappropriate homophobic comments and forces players to go through hazing rituals.

The Bully Player is a serious detriment to the overall enjoyment of sports. There is an aura of entitlement that is present in every aspect of his role. He is arrogant beyond measure, assuming his talent on the field is worthy of unconditional praise off it. He treats others in a condescending manner, only because he is able to succeed on the court. The majority of players do not want to associate themselves with this type of character; however, the attraction is too difficult to ignore. Bystanders even find themselves caught up in the fracas not being able to make right choices over wrong. To be a Game Changer is a goal of every athlete. It would even be better if the goal of every athlete were to be an Upstander as well.

STRATEGIES AND TACTICS: WHAT TO DO ABOUT THE BULLY PLAYER

- Know what kind of bully you are dealing with.
- Do your best not to engage the bully—defending yourself is appropriate.
- Don't take what is said personally.
- Do not put yourself down.
- Let an adult know about what is going on.
- Adults, do not have a private meeting with the bully and target, ending with "let's shake hands."
- Encourage others to stand up.

ENDNOTES

1 http://www.nasponline.org/resources/factsheets/bullying_fs.aspx

2 Ibid.

3 Ibid.

4 Ibid.

5 Olweus Bullying Prevention Program.

6 Ibid.

7 http://www.cdc.gov/healthyyouth/yrbs/pdf/us_overview_yrbs.pdf

CHAPTER 9

The Bully Coach

One man practicing sportsmanship
is far better than 50 preaching it.
—Knute Rockne, Legendary Notre Dame Football Coach

Coaches play a critical factor in a player's life. Most of them coach for the love of the game: they want to instill passion as well as offer important life skills. They help players set a standard of excellence, identifying a goal and then working hard to achieve it. When it comes to relationships, players often cite some of the most influential adults in their lives as being their coaches. Even though a coach may be remembered as being tough, he is recalled in the spirit for which he stood in their life. However, being a successful coach has the potential for becoming a slippery slope.

There are numerous factors needed to be an effective coach. Understanding the game is first and foremost. The ability to develop a game plan is also essential. A coach's ability to maintain positive relationships with her players is also instrumental. However, the importance of winning cannot be easily downplayed. Although players are aware that losing comes with any sport, it is never fun when it becomes a regular occurrence. Even in recreational sports, winning does make its mark. Players want to win. Coaches want to win.

Coaches have a tremendous amount of power within their hands. The lives of young athletes are at stake each time that players take the court or the field. Coaches have the ability to influence whether sports are enjoyed or hated. For many players, the decision to continue playing rests at the feet of their coach. It just takes one bad coach to ruin a sport for a player. Most coaches respect this responsibility by balancing their drive for success with an ability to connect personally with their players. The good coaches get kids excited about sports. The bad ones discourage kids. A good coach can keep kids' interest in sports alive, while a bad one kills it in an instant.

STATISTICALLY SPEAKING...

1993 Minnesota Amateur Sports Commission (MASC): Found that 45.3 percent of kids surveyed said they had been called names, yelled at, or insulted by coaches; 21 percent said they had been pressured to play with an injury; 17.5 percent said they had been hit, kicked, or slapped; 8 percent said they had been called names with sexual connotations; and 3.4 percent said they had been sexually abused. This final number is very conservative because not many will admit it.[1]

2003 Study by Dr. Stephen Joseph at the University of Warwick: Verbal abuse can have more impact upon victims' self-worth than physical attacks, such as punching, stealing, or the destruction of belongings." Verbal attacks such as name-calling and humiliation can negatively affect self-worth to a dramatic degree. Rather than helping them to "toughen up," 33 percent of verbally abused children suffer from significant levels of post-traumatic stress disorder (PTSD).[2]

2005 UCLA Study by Jaana Juvonen, PhD: Demonstrated that there is no such thing as "harmless name-calling." Sixth graders who had been victimized felt humiliated, anxious, angry, and disliked their school more. What's more, the students who merely observed another student being bullied reported more anxiety and disliked the environment to a greater degree than those who did not witness any bullying.[3]

2008 National Alliance for Youth Sports survey of coaches, parents, and administrators:

- 29% witnessed a physical altercation involving coaches, parents, or officials.
- 74% saw a coach yell at a child for making a mistake in a game.
- 53% occasionally witnessed a coach arguing with another coach, official, or parent at a practice or game.
- 48% had a child quit a sport because he didn't like the coach.[4]

THE PARENT COACH

There are numerous opportunities to coach. The largest group of coaches involves parents who volunteer their time. Town recreation departments typically do not have enough coaches and rely on volunteers to serve in this capacity. These coaches are usually parents (albeit not necessarily experts) who give their time graciously. The commitment is reasonable without too many expectations: parents have an opportunity to connect with their child and help other kids at the same time.

As players age, however, many of them want a more competitive experience, so they want a more competitive coach. Options to play on select travel teams become available at this stage. Organized programs like Little League, Cal Ripken, PAL, UK Elite, and Pop Warner also become options. The more exclusive teams require tryouts with selections being made for those players who are deemed qualified to join. There are even different levels of competitive teams. Some teams refer to themselves as *elite* or *select*, or the teams might be categorized as A-level, B-level, and C-level teams.

Outside of middle/high school athletics, there are few professionally-trained coaches. There are a number of parents who played sports, but who lack the necessary professional qualifications. They volunteer to coach with their own child on the team for a number of years. These coaches learned how to play during their youth from a certain style of coach. Many of them possibly played in high school with relatively few having played in college. These parent coaches have an enthusiasm for the game, thus creating a great connection with their own child. It's a huge component of the parent-child relationship, and affords some very memorable life experiences. Most of these parents are very well meaning and want to do their best; however, they receive very little training and direction with regard to the sport or coaching. They rely on their own personal experiences, often mimicking what was role modeled to them. Unfortunately, it is often an "old school" approach.

Although some towns require coaches to be trained in some type of program, these programs usually cover very little information in a limited amount of time. For instance, Rutgers University offers their SAFETY Clinic (Sports Awareness for Educating Today's Youth) to volunteer coaches. It is a three-hour program that meets the "Minimum Standards for Volunteer Coaches Safety Orientation and Training Skills Programs" (N.J.A.C. 5:52) and provides partial civil immunity protection to volunteer coaches under the "Little League Law" (2A:62A-6 et. seq.)[5]. In order to be a volunteer coach, coaches in that location must take this training; however, most of the training focuses on safety, not necessarily the training needs of players.

Using parents to volunteer as coaches is appropriate. But when did it become an accepted practice to allow novices to instruct our youth? How many schools allow the volunteers of the Parent-Teacher Association to step into one of their classrooms to instruct students? Being a coach requires knowledge of age-appropriate abilities. The ability to be aware of physical skills, along with an understanding of emotional development is also important. By minimizing the significance of these skills within sports, the system contributes to a culture that allows inappropriate approaches to be used. Without the checks and balances needed to direct these coaches, our youth can be exposed to bully coaches. In addition, it further exacerbates the limited boundaries created between coaches and parents. These volunteer coaches do not have the appropriate training on how to deal with parents.

THE EMPHASIS ON WINNING

Vince Lombardi, the famous Green Bay Packers coach, once said, "Winning isn't everything, it's the only thing." For coaches, winning provides an interesting quandary. Numerous efforts are made in the younger years by coaches to focus on the enjoyment of the game. As players get older, the pressure begins to mount because winning becomes more of a priority. Parents pay significant dollars to place their player on competitive teams. Winning is the most transparent gauge used to determine ability and growth. Bullying in sports revolves around winning, in particular from the coach's standpoint. Winning does not have to be the top priority, yet it often is. Most coaches agree that winning isn't everything, but what really matters is having the drive to win. However, our society focuses on winning as the desired result that places that same expectation in sports.

Winning is so important now that over the past couple of decades leagues distribute trophies for just participating in sports. In an effort to make everyone a winner, trophies are handed out just for showing up. Losing is downplayed. This approach is neither reasonable nor realistic. There is nothing wrong with losing. Yet this formula demonstrates the value of winning with the need to ensure that the feeling of victory is provided to each individual, regardless of effort.

WHAT ABOUT YOU?

How important is winning to you? If you are a coach and your team wins, does that mean you are doing your job better? Does it make you a more effective coach? Similarly, when your athletes lose, does that mean you are failing? Are the losses evidence of your incompetence? How do you view winning? Is winning and all that it means more important than the mental health of your players? Would you place your needs to be successful over the needs of your young athletes?

Winning is a cornerstone of every aspect of American society. Some coaches believe their win-loss record is more important than the process of participation. Winning outshines the value of character development and the safety of their athletes. They believe that any failure is reflective of their coaching skills. This sentiment is obvious in professional post-game interviews. The coach sits in front of a microphone answering questions. The first statement out of his mouth following a loss is "The loss sits on my shoulders. I did not prepare my team to play today." Since most coaches lack training, they use professional coaches as their role models. This formula reinforces an amateur coach's thought process, validating his sense of responsibility to his players.

Unfortunately, when coaches subscribe to this creed, the outcome generally is not a supportive environment. When coaches put the need to win in front of their athletes' well being, serious problems can develop. Interactions with coaches who believe that the end always justifies the means can create long-term damage to athletes. When winning is more important to the coach than the experience of the athletes, it's very likely a culture has been created for a Bully Coach.

THE THIN LINE

Coaches walk a very thin line when it comes to their focus on winning, and they use a variety of strategies to accomplish that win. For example, some coaches are great role models who seem to generate positive affection toward their players. These coaches identify growth opportunities and win by seizing those opportunities. Other coaches win by screaming and intimidating their players. Coaches can be nonchalant, showing up just before game time and allowing everyone a chance to play without any structure in place. Or they can live vicariously through their players, having a hard time separating their present from their past.

Since many coaches are not professionally trained, they rely on their own personal experiences and frequently emulate what they learned from their coaches. But times have changed, and the methods that were acceptable 20 years ago may not be considered to be correct today. For example, in the past, it was commonplace to use random running as a punishment or sitting players who made errors on the bench. It was appropriate to use scare tactics such as yelling to get players to perform. A coach could grab a facemask, pulling a player toward his face and yelling at his lack of performance. Those were all standard behaviors.

FUN QUIZ: WHICH HEADLINE IS FICTION?*

1. A t-ball coach pays one of his players to hit his autistic teammate with a baseball to take him out of the game.

2. An assistant youth football coach rushes the field and assaults an opposing player for making a late hit on his son.

3. A coach of a football team of 11-year-olds shoves an opposing player in the helmet during the post-game handshake.

4. A New Jersey youth baseball coach and councilman is suspended for using profanity in front of his team.

5. All of the above.

6. None of the above.

*Answer is at the end of this chapter.

But times have changed. A lot has been learned about the power of positive coaching styles. Protocols are being put into place to better understand winning. Role modeling behavior has a tremendous impact on athletes. Coaches that scream defend their approach as good, solid coaching. They are often referred to as "old school." They rationalize their approach as making athletes mentally tougher and physically stronger. They might be heard saying, "If you baby them, praise them too much, or falsely build self-esteem, then you're really hurting the kids because you're making them weak." They can also be heard saying, "Putting players down is a strategy to learn how tough it is out there. That way, they can prove me wrong. Deep down, I really do care about them." Another might say, "This is a very hard, dog-eat-dog, competitive world where bosses yell at their employees. Everyone has to learn to deal with getting his self-esteem regularly stomped upon. I'm just teaching these kids how to handle it now!"

Whether the approach of the "old school" is accepted or not, there is some truth about the desired outcome. It *is* important for young people to learn about overcoming adversity. Being able to deal with a tough boss is certainly an advantage. Corporate executives do complain that young professionals have a sense of entitlement. However, in order to learn these valuable lessons, does a coach need to demean his players? It is a very thin line indeed.

Coaches must become aware of the power of their words. Young athletes look up to their coaches as role models. They are individuals of inspiration. Coaches' words can transform a player. They can motivate a team to accomplish more together than they ever could on their own. Some of the greatest speeches by coaches can now be seen daily on YouTube. Coaches such as John Wooden, the retired basketball coach from UCLA, are truly inspiring. Wooden's words are legendary and repeated by coaches everywhere frequently. Mike Krzyzewski, head coach for Duke basketball, has a book titled *Beyond Basketball: Coach K's Keywords for Success*. Herb Brooks, the U.S. Olympic hockey coach who led his team to an unexpected gold medal in 1980, has a game time speech that was immortalized in the movie *Miracle*. When coaches understand the influence of their words, they transfer their energy onto the players, getting them to perform unbelievable deeds.

The same transfer of energy occurs when coaches choose to use inappropriate strategies with their words (however, it's an adverse reaction). When coaches scream at their players in front of others, belittling them in an attempt to motivate them, it is their words that leave painful memories embedded in a young player's life. Coaches who use their words to curse simply provide permission for their players to do the same. Coaches who place blame on players become a role model for the inability to accept responsibility. Coaches who use guilt to motivate players can cause lifelong damage to their athletes.

A PLAYER'S NIGHTMARE

Going into high school I was a standout athlete with high confidence. But after my freshman year, I started to lose interest. It just wasn't fun anymore. I hated practice because I was always worrying about messing up and being embarrassed by the coach. In games I worried about what he would do or say if I made a mistake, so I became less aggressive. When I thought I did something right, he thought it was wrong, and when I tried to work hard and gain his approval, it was never good enough. It got to the point where I was making up excuses to get out of practice, and I even hoped I would be benched so I didn't have to worry anymore. I knew the coach was tough, and I have no problems doing extra work or having someone push me to do better. But when he gets in my face, calls me out, embarrasses me in front of the team, and has a problem with me every day it makes me question why I still play. I used to play to learn, compete, be with friends, and have fun. Now I can't wait for the season to be over, and practice is always the worst part of my day. I don't tell anyone how it affects my motivation and confidence because it's football, and everyone complains about the coach. You just have to quit or accept it.[6]

—Anonymous Player

Most of the time coaches are completely unaware of the power of their words and how they can affect an athlete's life. Coaches can be heard on the sidelines cursing, dropping "F-bombs" before, during, and after a game.

ACTUAL HIGH SCHOOL BASEBALL COACH

Following a varsity baseball game in the spring of 2013, a head coach was overheard on a school bus yelling at his players using the "F-word" at every moment possible. An anonymous parent wrote to the coach imploring him to minimize the screaming and the use of foul language. Instead of acknowledging to the players the following day the inappropriateness of his words, he chose to threaten the team. Instead of being open to the power of his words, he chose to place blame on the players. He was heard saying, "If you don't like my screaming, then you don't have to play for me."

Where else in our civilized culture would we allow an adult to use language in that capacity and get away with it? Who in their right mind would allow their boss to curse at them continuously, simply accepting it as normal? How many of the coaches would be allowed to continue their role as a teacher in the classroom if they used that same type of language toward their students? These words used in sports would not be an acceptable form of communication in any other industry or profession. Why then do we accept them here?

CHARACTERISTICS OF THE BULLY COACH

A key contributor to the bully culture in sports is the coach because the greatest impact of negative behavior begins at the top, trickling down. Unfortunately, most coaches are not able to acknowledge their own bullying behavior. Just like Bully Players, Bully Coaches come in varying degrees. Typically, they also reflect the three components of bullying: aggressiveness, repetition, and creating an imbalance of power. Here the three common types of Bully Coaches are identified: old school, screaming monster, and know-it-all. However, be aware that Bully Coaches can have some or all of the other behaviors present at any time as well. One of the most popular types of Bully Coach is called the old-school coach. This type of coach runs practices and games in a strict, no-nonsense fashion, often benching or chastising players for mistakes. The core philosophy is that the only way to have fun in sports is to win. This type of coach often creates an intense amount of insecurity in athletes by using intimidation, fear, and manipulation.

The second type of Bully Coach is the screaming monster. This coach also takes winning seriously, but he recognizes the situation and knows better. The core philosophy seems to be that when my voice is raised, it's because of the excitement, and I want you to play well. This type of coach believes he has carte blanche to berate officials and to verbally abuse players during the game. Inappropriate language spews from his mouth, dropping "f-bombs" and demeaning anyone in his path, especially after a loss. Once the competition is over, with time passing from a loss, the coach is all sweetness.

His kindness resumes with his light-hearted nature. This type of coach seems to have a dual personality, creating a sense of uncertainty in athletes.

The third type of Bully Coach is the know-it-all. This coach wants everyone to know what an expert he is and that his way is the only way to do things if they want to win. This coach wants to win, but if the team loses, it's because they didn't listen to the coach. It's their fault for not paying attention and doing what the coach wanted. His core philosophy relies on the team following instructions and doing what is expected of them. This type of coach creates frustration in his players. Players do not want to let their coach down, but they may not be comfortable doing what the coach asks. They are afraid of speaking up when their coach "knows everything."

EVERYONE RECEIVES THE ATTENTION

The Bully Coach not only focuses his bullying behavior toward players, but also toward officials, other coaches, the administration, and even parents.

Officials are a crucial part of any game. The results of the entire game may hinge on what an official says or does. A common maxim is that "referees are never noticed during the game unless a bad call is made." Let's face it—questionable calls *do* happen all throughout sports, but particularly in youth sports. Unlike the professionals, amateur officials do not have the ability to review a videotape to ensure that a call is made correctly. Bad calls are part of every game. Sometimes they go in one team's favor, and then the next time, they go in another team's favor. When coaches throw their hands up in the air, yelling at perceived missed calls, it gives every one of the players permission to do the same thing. As the coach loses control, his emotions take over. Frankly, it is an embarrassing event to witness. It's not wrong to want fair calls along with fair play, but there are times when a bad call has changed the outcome of some very important games. No official wants to be on the end of such a call, particularly knowing he made an incorrect assumption that impacted the game. Yet screaming at an official is not the type of behavior to be modeled to kids.

Bully Coaches also target other coaches. Amazing as it may sound, this behavior often takes place in high school sports. Some schools have a very small pool of athletes from which to choose. In some situations when a player doesn't make a particular team, another coach gets wind of it and then invites that person to join their particular sport (say from track to baseball). In other situations, a coach will use unnecessary comments about other coaches in order to encourage a player to join their sport. They put down other coach's philosophies in order to gain an advantage with a potential player. In many schools, sports reign supreme, with the individuals who lead these teams getting special treatment within the school community. Jealousy takes over when some sports seem to be favored over others.

Coaches can also target other faculty members, even administrators. In many high schools across the country, coaches make a higher salary than the average teacher. In a few situations, they even make more than the principal. In these situations, there is a literal financial imbalance of power, which can contribute to the bully culture within the school. Coaches know they are making more money with a higher profile within the community. Other faculty are aware of that visibility, which demonstrates priorities within the school district.

As for parents and the Bully Coach, this relationship can be a source of real problems. Parents love their children, and they believe they know what is best for them. Parents are active participants in the sports scene with expectations of how situations will play out. They have values that impact their personal opinions. Some coaches communicate extremely well with parents. They know how to facilitate and manage this component of youth sports. On the other hand, there are coaches who wield power with a sense of authority and have tremendous reputations with egos to match. Their success record consists of state championships and a powerful network to get players onto teams at the college level. Parents are aware of this fact and willing to accept certain types of behaviors from coaches. Few individuals challenge a coach's authority. Those who do challenge the coach, may receive a proverbial "death sentence" from the town. Not only do these situations become public, but other players and parents count on that coach to attract the attention of top-ranking college sports programs, so they may put up with anything to achieve that goal.

Bully Coaches are in each of our communities. They walk in plain sight and are cheered by fans. Their tactics are ignored because they deliver wins, keeping their teams on the path to victory. They use intimidating strategies and humiliate players within the context of providing "tough love." Google "Bully Coach" and hundreds of weblinks will appear. It is not an isolated occurrence, but is happening in every town across the country. These coaches continue to be allowed to use these methods, believing their approaches are appropriate. They lack the ability to understand that their system is no longer acceptable. It borders on inappropriateness. However, for most coaches a subtle paradigm shift is all that is needed. Striving for excellence and encouraging players to reach their potential are both necessary to maintain within sports. The use of profanity, humiliation, and intimidation tactics is no longer an appropriate method, and coaches must be called out for that behavior.

STRATEGIES AND TACTICS: WHAT TO DO ABOUT THE BULLY COACH

- Educate people that bullying by anyone is unacceptable.
- Discuss strategies with players and empower them.
- As a parent, offer to help resolve the issue, but respect your child's wishes.
- Turn adversity into an opportunity to learn how to self-advocate.
- Reach out to coaches to meet in person at a separate time.
- Ensure that a plan is created and follow up with the coach.
- If needed, reach out to the coach's supervisor (for example, athletic director/recreation director).

ANSWER TO FUN QUIZ

The answer is 6. None are fiction, they are all real occurrences.

1. A t-ball coach pays one of his players to hit his autistic teammate with a baseball to take him out of the game. September 2006 in Uniontown, PA.

2. An assistant youth football coach rushes the field and assaults an opposing player for making a late hit on his son. September 2006 in Stockton, CA.

3. A coach of a football team of 11-year-olds shoves an opposing player in the helmet during the post-game handshake. October 2008 in St. Louis, MO.

4. A New Jersey youth baseball coach and councilman is suspended for using profanity in front of his team. May 2008 in Rutherford, NJ

ENDNOTES

1 1993 Minnesota Amateur Sports Commission (MASC).

2 http://www.eurekalert.org/pub_releases/2003-04/uow-nrd041503.php

3 A. Nishina and J. Juvonen, and M. Witkow, *Journal of Clinical Child and Adolescent Psychology*, "Sticks and stones may break my bones but names will make me sick: The consequences of peer harassment," 34 (March/April, 2005), pp 37-48.

4 http://www.pelinks4u.org/articles/Kulikov-Hagobian1208.htm

5 http://youthsports.rutgers.edu/

6 http://www.sportpsychologytoday.com/youth-sports-psychology/how-bully-coaches-affect-athletes-mental-game/

CHAPTER 10

The Bully Parent

It is our choices ... that show what we truly are,
far more than our abilities.
—J.K. Rowling, Author of Harry Potter Series

FROM THE AUTHOR'S PERSPECTIVE

Dealing with the Bully Parent is the most challenging of the three. The Bully Player and Bully Coach each have a supervising component. A player answers to an adult, either a coach or a parent. A boss supervises a coach. However, parents do not have the same type of governing body to control inappropriate behavior. Most parents have the right intentions, but end up allowing their emotions to interfere. An opportunity is now present to supply parents with the needed support and direction.

Being a parent is not easy. There are no "user guides" to provide directions on how best to be a parent. There are no classes that can be taken to prepare for parenting. It's all trial and error. Most parents use three priorities as a guide for raising their children: they want them to have good health, be happy, and be successful. However, when it comes to sports, parents transform into a unique breed. Involvement in sports changes everything. Parents recall their own experiences from their own youth. They dream about lost opportunities they experienced, only to have a second chance with their kids. Some parents decide to raise their child to play a certain sport, focusing on it nearly every waking moment. The sacrifices that are made to create an elite athlete are justified, because the end results are fame and fortune. Parents register for numerous sports activities and pay large sums of money with expectations of certain rewards. Yet when plans do not go as expected, parents fail to recognize that their own behavior may have contributed to the problem because their emotions prevailed instead of logic or reasoning.

Parents drive their children to every corner of town to participate in the latest tournament. They compare notes with one another, competing to see who has grossed the most miles. Moms run up and down the soccer field yelling at their player. Dads sit in bunches criticizing the coach's strategies or playing time of their child. They complain about the bad calls from the officials, never thinking about the message it sends to their kids, the players. What a sight it would be to have someone stand up while this happens and say, "Shut up! Just stop talking. Sit down. Support your child. Enjoy the nice weather and be a role model. If you don't like the coach's decisions, strap up your cleats and do it yourself. Otherwise, please stop this nonsense."

Parents realize that participating in sports is good for their child's health, giving their child much needed exercise as opposed to playing video games. They are also aware that being an athlete is a quality that assists kids in developing positive friendships in school. Sports provide great life lessons, teaching players about the opportunities that come with overcoming adversity. In addition, parents want their child to be treated fairly on a level playing field. But mostly, they want their child to have fun. As their player develops from beginner to intermediate to advanced, parents transform as well in ways that are sometimes completely inexplicable. Not many parents can openly admit they have become a Bully Parent. They believe they have the best interests of their child at heart.

RETURN ON INVESTMENT (ROI): PAY-TO-PLAY

In the past 20 years, we've seen a "professionalization" of youth sports. Not too long ago, athletes were able to compete in multiple sports throughout the year. It was common for a player to spend the fall season playing football, winter playing basketball, and spring playing baseball. Today, the three-sport athlete is nearly obsolete. It may be possible during the younger years, but it becomes increasingly difficult as players age. Some point the finger at the growth of soccer in the country and their year-round approach to choosing one sport, forcing soccer players to commit to a team in the fall, winter, spring, and summer. Other sports soon followed such as baseball, which can now be played in the spring, summer, and fall. With this year-round approach, businesses that offer skill development in sports have sprouted up throughout the country. These are professional companies that provide coaching to players of all ages. They offer individual skill development, as well as the opportunity to compete on independent teams. They promote their services to parents, offering players the chance to chase dreams of college athletics. It is an expensive luxury that contributes to unreasonable expectations for parents and players.

The consumer mentality has infiltrated youth sports. Parents pay for their child to participate in any sport. Whether it's a nominal $60 fee for playing on a recreational team or the $3,500 fee that is paid for an elite travel team, parents are consumers with expectations of a return. Parents can select from a myriad of sports with varying levels of degrees and costs associated to each. The marketplace decides the rate with large sums of money changing hands. When parents decide to purchase the services of a youth sports program, there are now expectations that demand to be met. In business, it is called ROI (Return on Investment), in sports it's called pay-to-play. In youth sports, this ROI is complicated, as the results are not easily identifiable.

When an individual invests money with a financial institution, he meets with a professional to discuss strategies. Together, they set up a shared goal to make more money. In sports, parents have multiple (many unreasonable) expectations; however, they do not have the same opportunity to discuss them with the coach as they did with their financial planner. There may be an initial meeting with the coach where philosophies and potential issues are shared, but if something interferes with their expectation, parents may find themselves in an unpleasant situation. Their money is already "on the table." The only way they can insure their ROI is to confront coaches in such a way as to retain control of that investment. They have paid their money expecting their child to play.

Bob Bigelow, noted author of "Just Let The Kids Play" and former professional basketball player, discusses the adult-driven, professional business-like approach now present in youth sports. Although the book was released over a decade ago, the message is just as relevant today. In the drive to become more competitive and excel in sports, adults created an industry that identifies players as young as seven or eight and predetermines who is good and who can play. Gone are the days of pickup games and stickball in the streets. They have been replaced with elite teams, year-round travel programs, and tournaments that duplicate the professional sports arena.

Take this mindset and add an environment that includes competition, questionable officiating, coaches who yell, and other parents who want your child to lose. It's a recipe for disaster. The Bully Parent is growing in sports. It may seem strange to think that parents can be bullies; however, not only is it possible, but it often happens within sight of other adults. A Bully Parent often becomes overly emotional, verbally abusive, and even physically aggressive. There are numerous stories in the news about parents hurting coaches, parents inappropriately yelling at officials, and parents of one team confronting parents of another.

The Bully Parent can no longer be condoned: the problem must be addressed. Coaches constantly complain about parents. They become irrational, unreasonable, and demanding, all for the sake of their love for their child. The antics that they use border on lunacy. Parents confront coaches immediately after a game without the ability to walk to their car. Some parents send text messages with unreasonable expectations of hearing back immediately. When they don't, they email the coach copying the athletic director, vice principal in charge of sports, principal, superintendent, and president of the board. Parents aggressively run onto the field of play targeting another player. Obnoxious parents are heard screaming insults from the stands. In some states, parents are savvy enough using state bullying laws to target coaches, claiming they are bullying the players. In reality, the parent is upset over playing time.

CROSSING THE LINE

An online article written in 2008 by Brooke de Lench, "Out-of-Control Parents in Youth Sports: Symptom or Disease?[1]" highlights the growing concern of parents' behavior in youth sports. De Lench shares that part of the problem stems from parents who do the following[2]:

- Use youth sports to gratify their own egos.
- Are not able to cope with the emotional ups and downs.
- View youth sports as a zero sum competition with other parents.
- See the time and money spent as an investment.
- Believe that lower standards of behavior apply to youth sports.
- Have a hard time giving up control.[3]

Given what de Lench identifies in the sidebar, it makes sense why there are so many parents who seem to cross the line and become a Bully Parent. Parents often end up living vicariously through their children. They have their own regrets, identifying mistakes that were made in their lives. They will do everything they can to have their children not make those same errors. Unfortunately, these parents are unable to realize that those mistakes helped form their character as individuals. Without them, they cease to be the people they have become.

Bigelow states, "Parents are sometimes described as overgrown children who cannot keep their tempers in check. It's all part of an angry (overwhelmed, media driven) society prone to violence."[4] It is difficult for parents to be self-aware when emotions and the state of youth sports intersect. As parents sacrifice their lives (including other children), it's no surprise that they can be at their wit's end when they see their child is unhappy or not getting as much playing time as other players on the field. No one is immune to inappropriate behavior as parents overstep the line from being a spectator to a bully.

A recent conversation with a neighbor who is coaching his son's six year-old basketball team sheds some insight on this phenomenon. He was sharing a story about one of the players who is literally a heads-length taller than the rest of the team. In addition, his skill level is so much better that there's a clear differentiation between him and the rest of the team. He began a conversation with this player's parents about his ability on the court. He discovered this player was already working with a personal coach to better his skills. When he shared that news with his wife, the first thing she said was, "Should we get a coach for our son as well?" These types of situations are real. They start taking place when kids are barely in elementary school.

THE TARGETS

The most common target of the Bully Parent is the coach or the official. Other players can be subjected to inappropriate comments from the Bully Parent, too. In some situations, the Bully Parent is also the coach, with the bullying behavior directed toward his own child. Perhaps his child is acting inappropriately, being a bad sport, or not living up to expectations.

A PERSONAL EXPERIENCE

I was coaching a team with a player who had very poor sportsmanship. After getting ejected from his second game, I met with his parents to discuss his behavior. The league director suspended him for three games and when he returned I explained to his parents that I would keep a very close eye on him. If at any time I believed he was on the verge of inappropriate actions, I would keep him on the bench. The player and both parents agreed to my conditions, and the season progressed.

During the state semi-final game, the player showed up to the pre-game agitated and not in an appropriate state of mind. I made the decision to start another player, and sure enough his reaction reinforced my decision. He cursed, became angry, and I asked his mother to sit next to the dugout. His father started pacing back and forth in the stands.

We were down by a couple of runs when I decided to replace the pitcher. As I made the switch, the father noticed that his son was going to stay on the bench and started screaming and threatening me. I did my best to ignore him, but his behavior was embarrassing and shameful. The umpire looked at me and asked if the police needed to be called. Another father approached him to calm him down, and I asked for the game to proceed.

We eventually lost the game and gathered as a team in centerfield for a brief meeting. I did my best to focus and prepare for the following week's tournament, but I knew what was coming. As the team left the field, the father raced towards me, with my son at my side, screaming and yelling about what an awful coach I was and that I was showing my "true colors." He kept making comments about me, the players on the team, and my son. I reacted to him and snapped. Another parent grabbed the fungo bat from my hand, while I waited for this father to pummel my face. However, another father grabbed him to pull him away from me. He kept yelling and cursing, while I kept saying that he needed to take care of his son. I reminded him that his son has behavior challenges, and I was following our agreement. He kept threatening me and making inappropriate comments about my son. The screaming match went back and forth as I walked to my car. Fortunately, no one was hurt, but my son was confused and cried when we got back to my car, and we drove home.

When the Bully Parent focuses her bullying behavior on other adults (coaches, officials, parents), it may come in a variety of forms. Yelling is the most common type of intimidation tactic. In some situations, parents interfere with the coach's strategies by openly challenging them. They enjoy "stirring the pot" by engaging other parents to get on board with a specific issue. Coaches' decisions during a game are challenged, creating an unreasonable environment. These confrontation tactics take the target off guard, making him become defensive. The Bully Parent also uses foul language, makes threatening remarks, and has a win-at-all costs mentality. He is likely to "coach" and "referee" from the sidelines, concentrating on failings rather than successes. He is a blowhard who diminishes everyone's enjoyment of the game. The behavior is a regular occurrence. It is witnessed by everyone present, including the players, coaches, officials, and other parents. No one confronts the Bully Parent, and he is allowed to get away with unacceptable behavior. However, when the Bully Parent is challenged, the environment gets extremely tense with emotions running wild. That's when police and the law might get involved.

When the Bully Parent directs her behavior toward her own player (child), the impact on the young athlete is life altering. These parents hide behind the guise of supposedly "developing character" in their child. They believe they are making their player "tough" by helping their athlete stay focused on her goals. This type of parenting is simply deplorable and those who witness it must summon the courage to stand up to challenge such behaviors. The Bully

Parent's outright abuse, screaming, and showing excessive disappointment when things are going wrong must not be tolerated. The Bully Parent's behavior teaches children about losing control, behaving abusively, and being outright rude when things don't go their way. It's certainly reasonable to maintain high expectations for our children, helping them to develop those skill sets. But the Bully Parent who pushes his son so hard that the child is visibly upset must be held accountable for his inappropriate behavior. It is one thing to encourage young players by offering constructive directions to improve, but it's another to degrade, use putdowns, and exploit negative reinforcement. The unforeseen consequences for the Bully Parent may be that his own child withdraws from the sport. Another consequence might be that fewer people will be willing to volunteer for coaching and official positions. Given today's litigious society, there could also be an increased risk of legal action.

STRATEGIES AND TACTICS: WHAT TO DO ABOUT THE BULLY PARENT

- Stand up: be firm, but not confrontational.
- If needed, stand up with others.
- Utilize school/town (coaches, AD, administrators).
- Don't wait for someone else to intervene.
- Take the "high road."
- Say please and thank you.

ENDNOTES

1 Adapted from the book, *Home Team Advantage: The Critical Role of Mothers in Youth Sports* (HarperCollins 2006) by Brooke de Lench.

2 Ibid.

3 Ibid.

4 Bob Bigelow, Tom Mooney and Linda Hall, "Just Let The Kids Play" pg. 69.

CHAPTER 11

Types of Bullying in Sports

It doesn't matter if you can throw a wicked curveball if it's being aimed at someone; it doesn't matter if you're the star quarterback if you do it to show off and rule others. At some point, choices overpower abilities, and if you make the wrong ones, then even your abilities will fall into oblivion because you were dumb enough to abuse them.
—Author Unknown

One are the days of the conventional bully. The physical bully still serves as the most common representation of what a bully is, but now people realize that there are a number of different ways an individual can be cruel. Today bullies have numerous ways to torment their targets; however, bullying behavior falls into two generally different categories. The first category is direct bullying behavior when actions or words are aimed specifically at a target, and it is intentional in nature. Direct bullying might involve comments directed at a person about how he looks or acts. The second category represents indirect bullying. This behavior might not necessarily be aimed directly at an individual, but rather it is designed to have a negative impact on that person. Indirect bullying might involve spreading gossip about a person, knowing that others will pick up the rumors and spread them even further.

NATIONAL CENTER FOR EDUCATION STATISTICS[1]

Number and percentage distribution of students ages 12 through 18 who reported being bullied at school and cyber-bullied anywhere, by type of bullying or cyber-bullying: School year 2010–11.

TYPE OF BULLYING	NUMBER OF STUDENTS	PERCENT OF STUDENTS
Total bullied or not bullied	24,456,000	100.0
Bullied	6,809,000	27.8
Made fun of, called names, or insulted	4,303,000	17.6
Subject of rumors	4,469,000	18.3
Threatened with harm	1,232,000	5.0
Pushed, shoved, tripped, or spit on	1,923,000	7.9
Tried to make do things they did not want to do	804,000	3.3
Excluded from activities on purpose	1,355,000	5.5
Property destroyed on purpose	689,000	2.8
Not bullied	17,647,000	72.2
Total cyber-bullied or not cyber-bullied	24,411,000	100.0
Cyber-bullied	2,198,000	9.0
Hurtful information on Internet	884,000	3.6
Purposely shared private information*	263,000	1.1
Unwanted contact via e-mail	454,000	1.9
Unwanted contact via instant messaging	659,000	2.7

TYPE OF BULLYING	NUMBER OF STUDENTS	PERCENT OF STUDENTS
Unwanted contact via text messaging	1,073,000	4.4
Unwanted contact via online gaming	356,000	1.5
Purposeful exclusion from an online community	286,000	1.2
Not cyber-bullied	22,212,000	91.0

* This question is new in the 2010–11 survey.

NOTE: For bullying, "at school" includes the school building, school property, school bus, or going to and from school. Bullying and cyberbullying types sum to more than totals because students could have experienced more than one type of bullying or cyber-bullying. Detail does not sum to total population of students because of rounding and missing data. The population size for all students ages 12–18 is 24,690,000.

SOURCE: U.S. Department of Justice, Bureau of Justice Statistics, *School Crime Supplement (SCS) to the National Crime Victimization Survey* (NCVS, 2011).

There are five common types of bullying in sports: verbal, social, physical, cyber, and hazing. Each style has three levels of severity, with Level 1 being the least serious and Level 3 being the most serious type of behavior (see the table, Bullying in Sports Grid).

VERBAL

Verbal bullying behavior is one of the most common types of bullying. Comments are made toward a target using words to put another person down. Making the target feel inferior creates an imbalance of power. Language is used to gain power over a peer. The bully may claim that he was "just fooling around" or "just kidding," and that it was not done to be harmful. He might say that it was just "horseplay," which is part of being a teen. However, bullies generally use relentless insults that focus on physical traits or capabilities. This type of bullying is difficult to identify as it occurs when adults are not present. Although verbal bullying does not create physical damage, this form of bullying has long-lasting psychological damage on its target.

Level one types of behavior are the following: poking fun or teasing; using inappropriate language/cursing; providing nicknames that mock a player's ability; or placing blame when a player has made an error and placed the team in a losing situation. Level two comments are the following: threats of aggression; making fun of others in an attempt to humiliate them; or taunting and name calling with the intent to be hurtful. Level three verbal bullying includes the following: threats to harm someone physically; threats of retaliation; constant verbal abuse; or sexual harassment.

SOCIAL

Social bullying behavior occurs in the various locations and environments where bullying takes place. It uses social interactions and interpersonal situations to reinforce negative behavior. Level one identifies general bullying behavior that takes place in locker rooms, when players or team members gang up on one another, use talk trash, and exclude or isolate someone else. Level two behavior causes a target to be a part of an embarrassing situation where he can be humiliated, using types of racial or homophobic slurs, using obscene gestures, or setting him up to look foolish. Level three behavior occurs when a player is openly and actively shunned, and rumors are spread using various forms of media, including social media.

PHYSICAL

Physical bullying is undeniably the most common type of bullying that people think about when discussing bullying—not just in sports, but in all types of bullying behavior. This form represents the old school thinking of what bullying is, but with updated research, it is only one form of many bullying behaviors. Level one can be head butting, towel snapping, throwing objects, or taking another's possessions. Level two is an illegal use of the body, either by throwing an object at a player or using equipment to strike another person. Level three occurs when someone deliberately inflicts pain, holds someone against his will, locks him in a room, or uses inappropriate touching.

CYBER

Cyberbullying behavior is the fastest growing form of bullying, not surprisingly due to the rapid increase in Internet use. Technology has provided many wonderful ways to learn, grow, and connect. However, it has also opened a completely new and hurtful form of bullying and has allowed the past stereotype of bullying to completely morph. In the past, adults saw a bully as being an outcast, more physical than others, and easily identifiable. The cyberbully easily hides behind technology, is often considered a "good" student or leader by others, and can cause tremendous psychological damage toward his intended target. Level one behavior might involve making posts on Facebook, inappropriate tweets, and flaming (using technology to "flame" a situation). Level two is chat room gossip, harassing texts, and cyber stalking. Level three is texting embarrassing pictures, creating inappropriate websites, outing, or impersonating another person.

FREQUENCY OF CYBERBULLYING[2]

- The 2008–2009 School Crime Supplement (National Center for Education Statistics and Bureau of Justice Statistics) indicates that 6% of students in grades 6–12 experienced cyberbullying.

- The 2011 Youth Risk Behavior Surveillance Survey finds that 16% of high school students (grades 9-12) were electronically bullied in the past year.

- Research on cyberbullying is growing. However, because kids' technology use changes rapidly, it is difficult to design surveys that accurately capture trends.

- Overall, females (22.1%) are more likely than male (10.8%) students to be electronically bullied.[3]

- 88 percent of teens reported seeing people being mean or cruel on a social networking site.[4]

- 43% of teens reported that they have experienced cyberbullying.

- 20% of students admitted to cyberbullying others.

- Only 23% of teens reported being cyberbullied by someone they did not know.

- 45% of teens say that parents should tell their kids that cyberbullying is wrong.

- 27% of teens report that their parents have no idea what they are doing online.

STUDENTS ONLINE

- 75% of teens (ages 12-17) have a cell phone (including 58% of 12-year olds).

- 27% of teens with cell phones use them to go online.

- 95% of teens go online.

- 80% of teens who go online use social networking websites.[5]

HAZING

The final type of bullying behavior is hazing, which was discussed in greater detail in Chapter 5, "Causing Harm." Level one forms of hazing are forcing players to march in a line, making certain that players carry other player's bags, and making players stand against a wall for a certain period of time as part of an initiation. Level two includes taking the clothes off someone, providing physical evaluations, and writing on bodies. Level three consists of beatdowns, slut lists, swirleys (putting someone's head into a toilet and then flushing), and holding a person in the shower against his will.

BULLYING IN SPORTS GRID

	LEVEL 1	LEVEL 2	LEVEL 3
Verbal	Poking fun Inappropriate language Use of nicknames Placing blame	Threats of aggression Making fun of others Taunting Name calling with intent	Threats to harm Threats of retaliation Verbal abuse Sexual harassment
Social	Locker room Ganging up "Talking trash" Excluding/isolating	Embarrassing comments Types of slurs Obscene gestures Set up to look foolish	Shunning a player Rumors through media
Physical	Head butting Towel snapping Throwing objects Taking possessions	Illegal use of body Throwing at a player Striking with equipment	Deliberately inflicting pain Holding against will Locking in a room Inappropriate touching
Cyber	Posts on Facebook Inappropriate tweets Flaming	Chat room gossip Harassing texts Cyber stalking	Embarrassing pictures Creating hurtful website Outing Impersonating
Hazing	Marching in line Carrying players bags Standing against wall	Taking clothes Physical evaluations Writing on bodies	Beatdowns Slut lists Swirleys Holding in shower

STRATEGIES AND TACTICS: WHAT TO DO ABOUT CYBERBULLYING

Make time to speak to your child about "cyberbullying" and set cyber safety rules and expectations —"Rule of Thumb":

- Do not do or say anything online that you wouldn't do or say in person.

- Do not reveal anything that you wouldn't say to a stranger.

- Never share passwords, embarrassing photos, or personal information— even with your closest friend or boyfriend/girlfriend.

IF YOUR CHILD EXPERIENCES CYBERBULLYING[6]

- Save the URLs of the location where the bullying occurred.

- Document it by printing the emails or web pages. This is helpful because sometimes the information is deleted.

- Determine your point of contact at the school for reporting cyberbullying.

- Provide copies of the URLs or printouts to your child's school.

- Document your correspondence with the school and record the response.

ENDNOTES

1 US Department of Education, *Student Reports of Bullying and Cyber-Bullying: Results From the 2011 School Crime Supplement to the National Crime Victimization Survey*, August 2013, pg. T1

2 http://www.stopbullying.gov/cyberbullying/what-is-it/index.html

3 *2011 Youth Risk Behavior Surveillance Survey*, http://www.cdc.gov/mmwr/pdf/ss/ss6104.pdf

4 A. Lenhart , et al. *Teens, Kindness and Cruelty on Social Network Sites*, (2011). Accessed online from http:// www.pewinternet. org/~/media//Files/Reports/2011/PIP_Teens_Kindness_Cruelty_ SNS_Report_Nov_2011_FINAL_110711.pdf.

5 http://www.pacer.org/publications/bullypdf/BP-23.pdf

6 Ibid.

CHAPTER 12

The Universal Target: The Umpire

Goaltending is a normal job, sure. How would you like it in your job if every time you made a small mistake, a red light went on over your desk and 15,000 people stood up and yelled at you?

—Jacques Plante, Goaltender

There is one group of individuals who easily unites all types of bullies in sports. When they do their job well, they are hardly noticed. If questions arise around their performance, however, everyone is quick to jump on the bandwagon and condemn them. They are, of course, the umpires, the referees, the judges.

The officials mediating the game have a thankless role, yet they offer the most effective governing methods to ensure that any game is played fairly. The officials take the time to learn the rules of the game and ensure that a fair experience occurs on the field of play. Everyone loves to complain about the referee, including the parents who scream from the stands about missed opportunities; the coaches on the sidelines who complain about unfair calls; and the players in the game who accuse the refs of not being aware of what is taking place. Even spectators feel free to call out the refs on their perceived mistakes.

POOR SPORTING BEHAVIOR INCIDENTS REPORTED TO NATIONAL ASSOCIATION OF SPORTS OFFICIALS (NASO)[1]

Every day in America and around the world, sports officials are physically and verbally harassed. Most incidents do not require police or medical assistance, but in some cases, the harassment turns violent.

NASO receives more than 100 reports annually that involve physical contact between coaches, players, fans, and officials.

As the world of sports has grown in the past few decades, so has the need for officials. The National Association of Sports Officials (NASO) maintains a membership of nearly 19,000 members from around the world. Founded in 1980, it provides advocacy for its members, including training seminars and benefits. The growth of sports has created a greater need for officials to effectively manage competition. The NASO is cognizant of this need and ensures that officials are better prepared for their responsibilities. However, the culture that promotes bully players, coaches, and parents collectively creates the opportunity for the referees to become a mutual target. With the increase of violence against officials, finding individuals to fulfill these refereeing roles is becoming more and more difficult.

There are moments in sports history when coaches and players have expressed their opinion of an official's call. For instance, on February 23, 1985, former Indiana University basketball coach Bobby Knight was in a highly emotional situation. The visiting Purdue Boilermakers took a quick lead of 11-2 within the first few minutes of the game. In a matter of one minute, the officials called three fouls on various IU players. Coach Knight went absolutely ballistic, screaming and cursing at the officials, which led to a technical foul. In rage, Knight grabbed a folding chair from the bench, throwing it across the basketball court to the shock and disbelief of everyone watching. This ugly incident became legend instantly with it being replayed over and over again. Unfortunately, this unsportsmanlike behavior was not limited to this situation. A number of other national incidents occurred leading up to a 2000 videotape showing Knight physically choking one of his players in a 1997 practice.

AN ATHLETE'S STORY—"SWEET LOU"

Lou Piniella is a former professional baseball player and manager. On September 18, 2002 in the bottom of the ninth inning against the Texas Rangers, there was a close play at first with the runner being called out. "Sweet Lou," as he was popularly known, came out to argue the call. The first base umpire immediately tossed him out after he threw his hat in disgust. Sweet Lou continued to scream in the umpire's face, kicking dirt at the same time. The first base coach momentarily restrained him, and then Sweet Lou ripped first base out of the ground. He threw it down the right field foul line twice, after imitating the umpire throwing him out. To date, no other coach has shown such animated rage in a baseball game.

AN ATHLETE'S STORY—"YOU'VE GOT TO BE KIDDING ME!"

John McEnroe is a former professional tennis player and current television analyst. Some of the greatest tennis ever played included him in the match. Yet, he is infamous for his ability to lose his temper during play with outbursts directed at the umpires. In 1981 during a first-round Wimbledon match, McEnroe disagreed with the lead umpire's call, arguing he had hit the ball inside the line. "You can't be serious man, you cannot be serious!" he roared. "That ball was on the line. Chalk flew up! It was clearly in. How can you possibly call that out?!"

With the fans applauding, the umpire awarded the point to his opponent. McEnroe continued his rant at the umpire, "You are the absolute pits of the world, you know that?" he said, receiving another point penalty. However, he went on to defeat his archrival Swedish-born Bjorn Borg in the final, earning him his first Wimbledon title and securing his rant as one of the most famous of all time in tennis.

Frustration is an obvious emotion to experience when a questionable call is made. Everyone participating simply wants the event to be fair. However, since human beings are involved, there are going to be times when some calls are incorrect. It happens all the time. But why do coaches and parents have to make disparaging comments in those moments? Why is it necessary to publicly challenge the authoritative person on the field? What is the message being taught to young players? When adults perform in this fashion, permission is granted to players to act in a similar way. The attempt to humiliate these central figures in sports is condoned. Although the power within this structure sits with the umpires, if nothing is done to restrict this behavior, the imbalance of power is given away. The coaches and parents try to get "inside the head" of the official in an attempt to have a future call go their way.

FUN QUIZ: WHICH HEADLINE IS FICTION?*

1. A parent body-slammed a high school referee after he ordered the man's wife out of the gym for allegedly yelling obscenities during a basketball game.

2. A father was charged with two counts of aggravated battery and one count of battery after allegedly charging onto the field and attempting to choke the game official.

3. A 13-year-old hockey player was charged with assault after punching a referee in the face, knocking him down.

4. A youth baseball coach was barred from coaching his 9/10-year-old Little League team after being criminally charged for pushing, shoving, and punching an umpire. The umpire had disqualified two aluminum bats prior to the start of a game based on a safety rule.

5. All of the above

6. None of the above

*Answer is at the end of this chapter.

Throughout time, officials have endured bullying of all sorts. "Kill the ump" has been heard for years from the stands at professional baseball games, but these days, it seems as if that phrase can be taken literally. In 2013, a 17-year-old actually killed a referee during an altercation that occurred during a soccer game in Salt Lake City, Utah. Out of anger over a penalty call, the player punched the referee in the face. What precipitated this outrage was that the player became upset when he was caught shoving an opposing player.

NASO has documented numerous reports of referees being verbally accosted and threatened before, during, and after games. Because of this fact, NASO has created grassroots efforts to address these types of situations in states across the country. Although many states do have laws in effect that can hold those accountable for their inappropriate actions, the problem is that they keep occurring. The current legislation is not deterring individuals from these verbal and physical assaults against the referees. In many states, the punishment is minimal compared to the severity of the exhibited behavior.

Parents often complain about their teenage player talking back to them. They get upset over being challenged on their decisions. They cannot believe the audacity of their teenager being so aggressive with their negative behavior. Ironically, these players are often the children of those parents who verbally accost the umpires at games. Monkey see, monkey do. The sooner this unacceptable behavior can be limited, the sooner there will be an opportunity to handle negative situations in a more appropriate manner.

ANSWER TO FUN QUIZ

The answer is 6: None are fiction, they are all real occurrences.

1. February 2004 in Pennsylvania

2. 2003 in Illinois

3. November 2002 in Ohio

4. April 2002 in Tennessee

ENDNOTES

1 *Poor Sporting Behavior Incidents Reported to National Association of Sports Officials*, NASO, n.d.

CHAPTER 13

The Game Changer Attitude (David and Goliath)

From what we get, we can make a living;
what we give, however, makes a life.

—Arthur Ashe, Professional Tennis Player

Sometimes, a moment occurs in sports that dramatically alters the course of a game or a season and it's simply miraculous. It might be a particular play that drives a team to victory, or a specific win over an adversary that seems to move the team to an entirely new level. It could happen in an instant or over the course of a few games. That moment or event often impacts the character of an athlete and the core of the team. It is the instant when fate comes alive, and it's referred to as a "game changer." These moments are created by an individual completing a remarkable feat, or a group of players who unite, thus altering the outcome based on their ability to achieve the impossible. Sometimes it's referred to as momentum, motivation, or even the sports gods, but the game changer drastically impacts the end result.

Babe Ruth was someone who changed the face of the game of baseball. He was bigger than the game, building the "house that Ruth built" as a NY Yankee in the Bronx. Broadway Joe Namath had his moment that changed the course of history in football when he predicted his team would win the Super Bowl. Michael Jordan not only changed the game of basketball, but also created a shoe brand larger than any clothing line in history. Martina Navratilova, John McEnroe, and Arthur Ashe were game changers in tennis. Tiger Woods changed golf. There are so many times in sports where a game changer helps force paradigm shifts.

AN ATHLETE'S STORY—KIRK GIBSON

During the first game of the 1988 World Series, the Los Angeles Dodgers were at home facing the Oakland A's. The Dodgers were down 4-3 heading into the bottom of the ninth inning as the league's best closer Dennis Eckersley took the mound. At the beginning of the game, Kirk Gibson, the team's renowned game changer, took himself out of the lineup due to severe pain in both legs. One leg had an injured hamstring, while the other had a swollen knee. Throughout the game, TV announcers Joe Garagiola and Vin Scully commented on his absence and speculated how the game would be significantly different if he were in the lineup.

Mike Scioscia, the current manager for the Los Angeles Angels, led the inning off with a pop out to shortstop Walt Weiss for the first out. As the catch was being made, Jeb Hamilton walked to the plate. During his time at bat, the camera panned to Kirk Gibson sitting in the dugout. Hamilton eventually struck out, leaving two outs in the bottom of the ninth.

Mike Davis walked to the plate as a pinch-hitter working the count to three balls and one strike. Then he drew a walk on the following pitch. Then the stadium broadcaster announced that Kirk Gibson was pinch-hitting, and the stadium erupted with fanfare. Gibson walked out of the dugout to a standing ovation. He grabbed some pine tar for his bat and took a few practice swings stepping into the left side of the batter's box.

The first pitch from Eckersley was a fast ball on the outside corner that Gibson fouled off behind the plate. His legs noticeably gave way as he stumbled out of the batter's box following his swing. The crowd in the stands were on their feet cheering him on in unison. The next pitch was also fouled off with the same stagger that occurred after the first swing. The count was zero balls and two strikes.

The next pitch was again fouled, a squib down the first baseline. His limp was very apparent as he ran down the baseline and then returned to pick up his bat. The next pitch was a ball for a count of one ball and two strikes. Another ball was fouled off, as Gibson continued to stammer after the swing. The next pitch was a ball to make the count two balls and two strikes. Mike Davis stole second base, getting into scoring position, while Eckersley threw ball three, leaving a full count for Gibson.

As the tension in the stadium mounted, Eckersley leaned in to get his sign, but Gibson called time, stepping out of the box to find his composure. Eckersley made his next pitch, a breaking ball down the middle of the plate, but Gibson was ready and simply threw his hands at the ball making immediate contact. The ball lifted off the bat and sailed 375 feet over the fence and into the right field stands for a two-run, game-winning, walk-off home run. The crowd went ballistic as he hobbled around the bases, with his right arm high in victory as he rounded first, then pumping his arms in triumph as he hit second base. The Dodgers' dugout emptied, and fans in the stands were jumping up and down with deafening cheers. He was greeted by his teammates at home plate winning the game 5 to 4. As pandemonium rocked throughout the stadium, it took him nearly five minutes to get from home plate to the dugout. Hugs and high fives were being thrown all over the place. Vin Scully was heard saying, "Gibson made the improbable and impossible, possible."

The crowd stayed in their seats as Bob Costas interviewed Gibson over what had transpired a few moments earlier. Kirk admitted the pain that he was feeling, having no idea what to expect. At the beginning of the game, he was in no position to help his team, but was sitting on the training table during the game when he heard Vin Scully mention he was missing from the dugout. He made a decision in that moment to have the manager Lasorda come back to talk with him. He told Lasorda that he was able to give him one at-bat and that he would go out there and give everything he had. Lasorda rolled the dice and came up with one of the greatest moments in World Series History. Gibson became the NBC Miller Lite Player of the Game with that one at bat. The Dodgers upset the heavily favored A's to win the World Series in five games 4-1. Many say that home run by Gibson was the key moment that created the overall advantage for the Dodgers.

The story of Kirk Gibson helps athletes learn about commitment, courage, and tenacity. At that moment in time, overcoming adversity was at the forefront of Gibson's mind. It is moments like these when the world of sports is at its best. These lessons can be shared with other athletes, using an authentic situation that resonates with each player to help inspire their own motivation. When these character-building moments occur, an attentive coach helps reinforce that teachable moment.

A game changer creates a paradigm shift that provides a perceptive change similar to what happened when David defeated Goliath. The biblical story is a classic, highlighting the underdog in the fight. It offers hope that transforms the impossible into the possible.

DAVID AND GOLIATH

The Philistines were gearing up for a war against the Israelites. The two armies were camped facing each other in a steep valley. The Philistines had Goliath, a giant of a man who constantly mocked the Israelites, challenging them to fight. The physical sight of the beastly man terrified King Saul and the Israelites. They feared their impending death. However, one day a young teenager named David noticed Goliath yelling words and threats at his people. He noticed the fear that was present in the people's faces and volunteered to fight Goliath.

King Saul was not immediately convinced that it was a good idea for David to fight, but after a lot of persuasion he relented, allowing the fight against the giant. David was most comfortable in a simple tunic, not heavy armor. He approached Goliath with a shepherd's staff, a slingshot, and a pouch full of stones. He acknowledged the size and power of Goliath, but he believed that his strong faith in God was more significant that anything Goliath had at his disposal.

As Goliath moved in for the kill, David simply grabbed a stone from his bag, placed it into his slingshot, and let it fly toward Goliath's head. As fate would have it, the stone found a hole in his armor sinking into his forehead. He fell face down on the ground. Being taken off guard, Goliath could not make sense of what had happened. David grabbed a sword thrusting it deep into Goliath's neck, killing him in an instant. David slayed Goliath, and the impossible became possible.

This popular biblical story represents the needed shift within bullying in sports. The setup between the two historical figures clearly demonstrated that the strength of Goliath was significantly more than David. Yet, through a shift in perception, David ended up unexpectedly victorious. It's the story of the small weakling overcoming brute, physical strength. It's about facing the odds and finding the inner courage to overcome the unexpected.

Just as the bully culture exists in sports, the magic of sports can be used as a game changer in confronting the challenges that exist. The values that sports promote are the same ideals needed to meet bullying head on. Not only does the makeup of sports create the bully, but it also has the ability to develop and raise awareness. Utilizing sports can be the necessary approach in reducing bullying behavior. There have been some incredible game changers in sports where athletes used their athletic training to stand up against bullying. Here are a couple such stories with a greater list provided in Chapter 17.

AN ATHLETE'S STORY—CARSON JONES[1]

Quarterback, Queen Creek High School
Queen Creek, AZ – December 2012

Carson Jones didn't think he was doing anything special when he asked his buddies on the Queen Creek High School football team in Queen Creek, Ariz., to help watch over a sophomore with special needs who was getting picked on by other students. The 18-year-old quarterback with a 4.3 GPA had no idea how his good deed would end up changing the life of Chy Johnson, whose neurological disorder limited her cognitive abilities to that of a third-grader. But Johnson, 16, went from being a bullied outcast to becoming one of the most celebrated kids at Queen Creek High.

Chy's mother Liz believed that had it not been for Jones, she would have pulled Chy out of school and home schooled her. She first met Jones years earlier while working as a teacher's aide in his elementary school. When Chy started coming home from her classes in tears, describing how kids were throwing trash at her and calling her names, Liz wondered if maybe the "wholesome, good-natured" Jones might be able to help.

Liz tracked down Jones through his Facebook page and asked if he could find out who was picking on her daughter. The next day, Jones found Chy sitting alone in the cafeteria and asked her to come sit with him and a group of other seniors on the football team.

Chy started spending time with Jones and the other players. Simultaneously, Jones approached her tormentors to get them to leave her alone. Not only did the bullying stop, but the players also made Chy an unofficial member of their team—walking her to classes, taking her to dances and parties, and even inviting her down to the sidelines during games.

Carson and the rest of the team's kindness wasn't lost on Chy. "They're my boys, and I'm their lucky girl," she said. "They're awesome."

AN ATHLETE'S STORY—KEVIN CURWICK[2]

Senior football captain, Osseo High School
Osseo, MN

Tired of seeing his classmates taunted on Twitter, Kevin Curwick created an anonymous Twitter account that would only spread good things in his school community. He was the mastermind behind @OsseoNiceThings that singled out the positive qualities and gifts of his classmates. He decided to change the conversation in his school by highlighting the nice instead of the nasty.

Although Kevin was not personally attacked, his friends were on the receiving end of several of these mean tweets. He realized how cyberbullying was affecting his schoolmates and wanted everyone to feel welcome instead. Eventually, he decided to step out of anonymity and became recognized by his football coach and made a team captain for his kindness and bravery to others. His idea has caught on at several other schools in Minnesota. By the way, the negative tweets that once flooded the community have disappeared.

Coaches, parents, and players often talk about the need for game changers. Although a large number of challenges have been presented in terms of the bully culture, behavior, and traditions, the positive elements within sports far outweigh the negative. In the chapters that follow, the focus will be on how players, coaches, and parents can contribute to the game changer attitude. In addition, strategies and techniques will be introduced in order to provide the necessary skill sets to implement the change.

STRATEGIES AND TACTICS: HOW TO CREATE A PARADIGM SHIFT

- Become aware of negative self-talk.
- Make a conscious decision to change anything that doesn't align with your values.
- Stop and think: Stop your current actions and think of the consequences.
- Create positive affirmations that support an end result you want changed.
- Develop an attitude of gratitude.

ENDNOTES

1 http://www.people.com/people/article/0,,20656400,00.html

2 http://www.huffingtonpost.com/2012/08/15/kevin-curwick-minnesota-osseo-nice-things_n_1784908.html

CHAPTER 14

Be a Game Changer: Become an Upstander

Treat a person as he is, and he will remain as he is.
Treat him as he could be, and he will become
what he should be.

—Jimmy Johnson, NFL Former Head Coach

Samantha Power, the current U.S. Ambassador to the United Nations, first introduced the word "upstander" in 2002. During her first commencement speech at Swarthmore College, she called upon students to become "upstanders" rather than bystanders in their post-college lives. It was a concept that caught on and is now used within anti-bullying education. It offers a reframing of the common bystander who simply watches and does nothing to the upstander, someone who has the courage to stand up against bullying behavior. According to the 2009 National Federation of State High School Associations, research provided by Bruce Howard and John Gillis identified that over 55% (nearly 7.6 million) of students in high school participate in athletics.[1] In some schools, the number is over 60%. There is no larger common denominator (without considering racial, ethnic or gender) in schools across this country. Sports provide the ideal opportunity for communities to pursue a shift in anti-bullying culture. Coaches and their players are in perfect situations to become game changers by engaging in the upstander role. Athletes look up to their coaches for direction and guidance. As coaches lay out their expectations for their players on the field, they can also add the expectation for their players to be upstanders off the field. Without exerting too much energy, coaches can help facilitate this important learning piece.

Athletes are accustomed to being encouraged by their coaches. They are used to a routine that includes physical conditioning, practicing skills sets, scrimmages to emulate game-like situations, and cool-down exercises. They have a well thought-out approach with various game plans, expectations, and strategies to create a level of excellence. This method is used in recreational sports and increases in intensity as a player develops into more of a competitive athlete. Coaches help create this environment because they command a level of respect unmatched by the classroom teacher. A culture of intolerance to bullying behavior can be created with leadership from the coach.

STAND UP!

An upstander is able to "stand up" to inappropriate behavior, so there are various components to empower athletes to become upstanders. In order to be able to correctly teach their players, coaches must serve as role models. They must train themselves by learning the anti-bullying language, strategies, and skill sets needed to intervene and then translate these same skills to their players. It doesn't take much time for coaches to introduce the upstander's strategies and then have players use role-playing techniques to practice their new skills. Coaches can even set up a "scrimmage," offering critiques of their upstander skills. After learning, athletes will be able to create a paradigm shift to help them identify and address various bullying situations. Once the players are confident with their upstander skills, coaches can explain the consequences that will take place if players choose to ignore these skills and still participate in hurtful behavior.

THE ROLE OF COACHES

Coaches can utilize their role in a player's life by helping them learn how to be an upstander. Since athletes have not been trained how to become an upstander, it is important to provide very clear and concise directions. There are three steps that are helpful in assisting players:

1. **Recognize the situation:** The first step to becoming an upstander is being able to recognize that a situation is inappropriate. It is important to know the difference between "horseplay" and bullying.

2. **Be responsible and empathize:** Once a situation is deemed to be bullying, the second step is to be responsible. Empathy is an essential component in the upstander mentality; it's important to want to do something about what is occurring.

3. **Do something:** The third step is to do something. It's vital to know what to do in a given situation and be able to act on the increased awareness.

To intervene and help someone who is being bullied does take someone of great character and courage, which is why coaches are in such a great position to do something with their players. Using the mindset of sports, coaches can take advantage of their athletes' natural drive, motivation, and commitment to excellence. Helping an athlete learn the difference between bullying behavior and other forms of interactions between people can provide a huge difference as to whether that athlete decides to intervene or simply be a bystander. The increased awareness and paradigm shift created for players can be extremely helpful in identifying negative behavior toward others.

Having students develop a sense of empathy and responsibility is an important component in helping empower them to be an upstander. Most young players are familiar with sympathy, but are not able to understand how it differs from empathy. People who are targets of bullying behavior really don't feel better when they know that someone feels sorry for them and what they've endured. They'd rather have someone empathize with them (for example, feel for them, even though they are not necessarily in the same situation) and by having those feelings, then help engage and distract the bullying behavior. Athletes are often fairly responsible individuals. In becoming an upstander, athletes are encouraged to identify bullying behaviors that are unacceptable and damaging to others. Those athletes who accept their responsibility will be able to stand up to the bullying perpetrators without fear of retribution. Generally, an athlete's mindset is built up by his conditioning, training, and coaching, so he is a natural choice for someone to defend against bullying.

NECESSARY SKILLS FOR AN UPSTANDER

The most significant component to help players become upstanders is whether or not they have the appropriate skill set in confronting and stopping such negative behavior. Taking some time to introduce appropriate skill sets to players may be the difference between confronting a student who is bullying others in a positive way and letting the bullying continue. Without a skill set, the athlete may do something detrimental with significant consequences. Their intention might have been in the right place, but they didn't have the appropriate training. They did take it upon themselves to do something about it, but ended up making the situation worse.

The skills needed to become an upstander include the following:

- The ability to have the courage to do the right thing.

- The knowledge to understand the difference between tattling and telling. (Tattling is about getting someone in trouble, and telling is about taking action to help the target.)

- The ability to go from tolerance to acceptance. (Tolerance is negative in nature, and acceptance promotes respect toward others.)

- The courage to dare the players to care (not only about their teammates, but other students as well).

In addition to being able to have an appropriate mindset in intervening in bullying situations, players must also be trained with tangible actions that they can practice. The specific strategies upstanders can use are the following:

- **Assertive statements** (being able to show the confidence and the ability to assert yourself toward the student bullying).

- **Fogging** (when the upstander takes on the same characteristics of the student being bullied in order to deflect what is being said).

- **Swarming** (when two or more players approach the student demonstrating bullying behavior in order to get it to stop).

- **Using the broken record approach** (for example, saying the same thing over and over again to hopefully demonstrate how their behavior is inappropriate).

- **Acknowledging** (when an upstander simply acknowledges a student who bullies as an outright bully and calls him out for his negative engaging behavior).

- **Have players take a "pledge"** and sign a team contract to help them take on an upstander role and agree to do so in writing.

Except for the last strategy, it is vital to also remove the target. That way the upstanders know that they have gotten the target out of the way. If there's no target, the student(s) who bully have no place to focus their negative behavior.

ENDNOTES

1   B. Howard and J. Gillis, *Participation in High School Sports Increases Again*. Indianapolis: National Federation of State High School Associations (NFSHSA), 2009.

CHAPTER 15

Be a Game Changer:
Become a Five-Star Coach™

Sportsmanship for me is when a guy walks off the
court and you really can't tell whether he won or lost,
when he carries himself with pride either way.
—Jim Courier, Retired Professional Tennis Player

Someone at a local high school was stealing practice jerseys from the athletic closet. They were popular among the students in the school, but necessary for practice. So the next year the coach ordered a set with "Property of Central High School" emblazoned on them. However, the thefts continued. The following year he ordered a new batch that had the imprint "Stolen from Central High School." But the jerseys still kept disappearing. The following year, the larceny finally stopped after he changed the wording to "Central High School 4th String."

—Author unknown

Coaches are a unique group of characters. Their skill set focuses on work ethic, achievement, and the pursuit of excellence. They have a strong drive that is only matched by the player, and they are often one of the most memorable people in a person's life. When someone has the opportunity to play for an exceptional coach, the bar is raised to such a standard that when he plays for a less than average coach, the letdown is often substantial. An exceptional coach is someone who creates a love for the game, treats players with respect, and forms an atmosphere of fun. A terrible coach is remembered for taking the enjoyment out of the game, screaming and embarrassing players, and only caring about winning. Ironically, the line between the two types of coaches can be extremely thin, which is why it is important for coaches to take a proactive approach in creating players with exceptional character. The Five Star Coach is that type of individual. In addition to offering direction on the physical components of the sport, the Five Star Coach simultaneously takes the time to teach athletes the elements of being a leader on and off the field. The lessons provided happen in real time for the athlete. They learn the importance of becoming an Upstander and the necessary skills alongside the drills needed to hit better, throw farther, and kick stronger.

TYPES OF COACHES

There are basically three types of coaches. The first is the professional coach, who has significant training and credentials that allows him to be compensated for his skills. These coaches (both male and female) can be found at the high school, college, and professional levels. The second is the volunteer coach who is the supervising adult helping out because she is able to give her time. This coach is the most common one seen filling in at the recreational level in towns throughout the country. The third is a hybrid of the other two called the professional-volunteer coach who has the skill set and ability, but offers his time for the love of the game. This may be the type of coach at an all-star or travel-level team. Regardless of the type of coach, all coaches generally emulate the role models they had during their youth. They willingly take on the same persona because the skills, strategies, and drills are familiar to them. Although the Internet does provide a vast amount of information, the mindset that coaches have is established years prior to becoming a coach. Therefore, what was generally acceptable 20 years ago in coaching is not necessarily reasonable by today's standards.

Coaches are really educators first. Their primary object is to teach players the sport. Doing that task requires preparation, planning, communication, time management, strategy development, and follow-through. The administrative aspect of coaching is somewhat simple. Coaches need to know the players' names, understand the positions, set the lineup, create a safe environment, and shake hands after the game. However, the true mark of an exceptional coach is the ability to take a sport and translate it into a guide to life's experiences. Creating teachable moments for players is an essential skill for today's coaches, which is why it is vital to ensure that coaches are prepared to take on that responsibility. It is even more important that the volunteer coaches without the necessary skills are provided the same vital training to ensure that they are successful.

Given the drastic emphasis on competition and winning at all costs, coaches must rethink and reinvent themselves. The current culture is no longer suitable. The behavior that is being promoted is currently doing more harm to our young players than good. Coaches have an obligation to lead by example, providing positive role models for our youth. Requiring coaches to have an understanding of physical development, emotional strength, and social skills is extremely reasonable. No parent would ever allow his or her child's teacher to lead a class without the appropriate certification and education. Why is the expectation in sports less?

THE FIVE-STAR COACH APPROACH

The Five-Star Coach approach is a powerful training experience that offers innovative coaching skills to coaches, as well as strategies designed to engage age-appropriate player behavior on and off the field. It is a sophisticated program that acknowledges the current challenges that coaches face. In addition, this program provides them with a skill set that is more appropriate for today's athlete. A coach willing to invest in becoming a Five-Star Coach gives parents and players an experience of a much healthier sports environment. The Five-Star Coach takes into consideration the desire to win and the competitive nature of sports. The program gives the coach the ability to incorporate character development and maximize life lessons. Here is a general explanation of the concepts of the program.

The four cornerstones for a Five-Star Coach are:

- Complete player experience
- Positive team environment
- Character building
- Academic achievement

Furthermore, the Five-Star Coach is able to understand and appreciate the rubric shown in the Five-Star Coach illustration below.

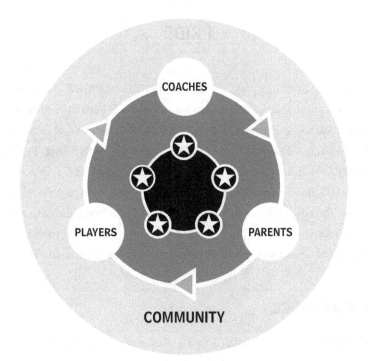

THE FIVE-STAR COACH RUBRIC

A Five-Star Coach appreciates the synergy that it takes to be an effective coach. Most importantly, the entire dynamic comes within the confines of the community. Whether the sport is a town recreation experience, a private travel/club, or a select or privately recruited program, sports involves the overall community. A coach is no longer an isolated individual acting alone without accountability.

A highly talented coach is able to connect with parents who buy into a particular program. Together, they create an atmosphere to reinforce the values of their players. Parents today are an active part of their player's lives, and those coaches who refuse to engage with parents in a healthy way will only alienate them. They will experience strong resistance from a vital component of coaching. If coaches communicate appropriately with parents and offer a transparent approach, parents will likely serve as advocates and create less havoc and challenges as the season progresses.

PRIDE

The Five-Star Coaching program utilizes the acronym PRIDE in communicating and teaching select skills to be an effective coach. Each letter of the word PRIDE coexists with a star. Once the coach masters each star, he is one step closer to being a Five-Star Coach. PRIDE stands for Performance, Respect, Integrity, Determination, and Excellence. When a Five-Star Coach coaches with PRIDE, he is in a unique position to communicate to his players and their parents. The coach's training not only consists of understanding the sport, but also receiving relevant preparation to foster an environment conducive to winning and a culture of sportsmanship, acceptance, and camaraderie.

PERFORMANCE

Performance is not just isolated to a philosophy of winning, but it's also about how athletes perform off the field. One of the central components of a successful coach is the ability to confront adversity. How coaches handle challenges identifies their central value system.

The Five-Star Coach understands that obstacles are really opportunities for growth. With the constant focus on winning, athletes often learn more about their play from losing or defeat. How a coach handles hardship demonstrates his or her true character. When it comes to bullying behavior, coaches are in an ideal position to address player development. Speaking about bullying provides a perfect opportunity for the coach to address the culture on the team, as well as the expected behavior off the field. Encouraging players to look for opportunities to become Upstanders is just as important a goal for an athlete as conditioning and training. When a coach determines that being an Upstander is a priority in the performance of an athlete, he creates an opportunity that encourages more appropriate behavior. The coach can also follow up and check in from time to time with the player to ensure that the goal of being an Upstander doesn't get lost over the course of a season.

An effective tool to assist the coach in identifying his own value system regarding performance is creating a Personal Coaching Statement (PCS). It's something that can be created and referred to before and after the season. A PCS is another tool to help lay the foundation for the coach. It is something that a coach can go back and refer to time and again to ensure that he stays focused on the larger picture of athletics. It's a useful approach that can help in a heated moment or when emotions can get the better of a situation.

Below is an exercise to help create the PCS:

I	II	III	IV
3 TO 5 GOALS THE TEAM CAN ACHIEVE THIS COMING SEASON.	3 TO 5 VALUES FOR THE TEAM.	3 TO 5 SKILLS THAT MAKE YOU AN EXCELLENT COACH.	3 TO 5 PERSONAL GOALS YOU WANT TO ACHIEVE REGARDING RESPECT ON YOUR TEAM.
1.	1.	1.	1.
2.	2.	2.	2.
3.	3.	3.	3.
4.	4.	4.	4.
5.	5.	5.	5.

When you are finished, circle the most important one in each column and write your statement on a separate sheet using the guidelines below:

I will accomplish (what you circled in column IV) using my (what you circled in column III) to achieve a team with (what you circled in column II) and in doing so, also attain (what you circled in column I) .

It may not initially come out grammatically correct, but work with it until it's something that resonates deep within you. There's no real right or wrong, but rather it creates an opportunity to put your thoughts, passions, and desires into a format that can be memorized and utilized to help guide and direct you as a coach. If you are having a challenge, feel free to drop me an email, and I will work with you to get something that works best for you. In addition, once you've completed your PCS, you can email me with your statement, and I will respond within 24 hours with your statement, name, and date in a nicely printed out format. My email address is coachrandy@projectnextgen.com.

RESPECT

Respect is an all-encompassing word for a Five-Star Coach: respect for players, respect for coaches, respect for officials, respect for fans/parents, respect for opponents, and most importantly, respect for the game. Each coach and player has a powerful internal belief system. These beliefs interact with external social customs that may conflict from time to time. For example, most young players by the time they get to high school know it is not nice to embarrass and tease another person. However, the team they play on has a tradition that makes the new players do things that are clearly unacceptable. Instead of notifying the appropriate adult, they choose to do nothing instead. Their internal belief system is compromised by the external social expectation. When a player's internal belief system matches the values and expectations of the coach, the odds for success increase immensely. It affords the coach the ability to teach lessons. In terms of bullying behavior, this component lets the coach match his beliefs with the overall plan for his players and team. He is able to clearly articulate the role of the Upstander and then teach his players the skills.

Some coaches believe the only gauge for success is winning. It is understandable to place winning as a top priority. However, if winning is the most important priority for a coach, he may have created a limiting belief of what it means to be a successful coach. A limiting belief is not about being right or wrong, but rather the limits it creates. If the belief system says that wins are what determine success, the coach is going to be limited by that thought. Every decision by the coach will be judged by whether or not the action will help create a victory. For those coaches who believe the only way to win is to scream, belittle, and openly challenge players in front of their teammates, they will act exactly in that fashion. The Bully Coach often has limiting beliefs that interfere with his growth. However, if coaches are willing to challenge the authenticity of those beliefs, they may discover opportunities to learn and grow.

Not too long ago, the coach that yelled, put players down, ran them hard, and called them out were the norm. In 2002, the movie *Junction Boys* starred Tom Berenger as the hard-nosed famous coach, Bear Bryant. The story is about Bryant's first summer in 1954 as head football coach at Texas A&M. Referred to as Bear, he takes his players out onto the scorched plains to see who survives. There's a powerful scene during the training camp when the players get a water break, and he decides to throw everything onto the ground and have them tough it out. It's a powerful scene, and anyone who played sports growing up in the 1970s-1990s probably experienced something to that effect. However, in today's times and standards, the assistant coaching staff or players would not tolerate this type of behavior.

Texas Tech has had its fair share of scandals in recent memory. First came football Head Coach Mike Leach in 2009 when he was fired after being accused of isolating a player in an equipment garage and a media room while he was sitting out practice with a concussion. An administrator from the university said, "His contemptuous statements make it clear that the coach's actions against the player were meant to demean, humiliate, and punish the player rather than to serve the team's best interest. This action, along with his continuous acts of insubordination, resulted in irreconcilable differences that make it impossible for Coach Leach to remain at Texas Tech." In September 2012, Head Basketball Coach Billy Gillispee earned a spot on the hot seat. Texas Tech players met with athletic director Kirby Hocutt with complaints about how Gillispie had held practices up to eight hours long, overworked injured players, and held players hostage while determining if he'd keep them on scholarship. Ironically, Pat Knight, one of the infamous Bully Coaches, offered his two cents on the story, neither vilifying Gillispie nor defending him when asked to weigh in on the situation. He stated, "I feel for the kids, and I feel for Billy…it's never a good situation to be in if you're the kids or the head coach because you're under the microscope."

There are many ways to earn and demonstrate respect as a coach. Yelling and pushing athletes in select situations is expected and appreciated by players. An old saying goes in coaching, "It's good when the coach yells at you, that means he or she still cares about you. It's when the yelling stops a player needs to be concerned." However, there are appropriate models and techniques that can be utilized without demeaning or humiliating a player beyond repair.

In Don Miguel Ruiz's book *The Four Agreements*, he identifies powerful principles to help empower an individual. The First Agreement is "be impeccable with your word." He says, "Speak with integrity. Say only what you mean. Avoid using the word to speak against yourself or to gossip about others. Use the power of your word in the direction of truth and love."[1]

The words a coach uses and his intent have a direct and powerful impact on the psyche and attitude of an athlete. Most coaches who use their voices to scream and yell often do so because of their passion and commitment to building a better player and encouraging their team to play at their highest level possible. An excellent coach understands the teachable moments that arise during practice and a game. The opportunity to learn and grow never stops. In some sports, the most effective way to be heard is by screaming since there is a lot of other commotion and noise occurring at the time. Some common phrases and words used by coaches are:

"I can't believe you did…."

"Where was your head when…."

"What were you thinking when…"

"What the hell is the matter with…"

"How many times do we have to go over…"

"I'm sick and tired of…"

There are a number of terms used to communicate with players to help improve their game. Some call it criticism, others put a positive slant on it and call it constructive criticism, while still others take it a step further and refer to it as positive feedback. However, what coaches are really offering is something that is called "positive direction." If the goal of a coach is to really develop their players, what they want to offer is direction. Every challenge that arises in practice or a game allows a coach to provide positive direction. Even the word direction offers a more meaningful approach than criticism or feedback. When a coach takes the approach of positive direction, the words, actions, and choices a coach makes are more effective in the long run.

Although it may seem easy in principle, creating this type of paradigm shift requires a conscious effort and opportunities to practice. As a coach incorporates positive direction, the shift begins with knowing the difference between sympathy and empathy. A coach who comes from sympathy may feel sorry for the player, but will be reminded of past experiences and create a disconnect because it's about the player and what has occurred with the team. A coach who uses empathy is able to remember what has taken place in the past, but have a deeper connection and remove the negative reaction and communicate in a more meaningful way.

Using the positive direction approach does not require significant change, but it will challenge the current process of most coaches. There is a four-step process that can be introduced and eventually change the current habits of the coach.

STEP 1: OBSERVE THE SITUATION

Most situations in sports often occur in a vacuum of emotions. Whether in practice, a game, or in a meeting, the emotions of a coach are a major component of how he/she thinks and acts. Experienced coaches have the ability to use their hindsight and background to anticipate the numerous challenges that may occur over the course of the season. However, there are unexpected moments that constantly keep them on their toes. When it comes to positive direction, the first step is to be able to observe a situation instantly without any type of emotional connection. It's something called "detached involvement." Being able to detach the emotion allows a coach to reflect on the situation in a more positive manner, without the possibility of making an inappropriate comment. Being able to "stop, breathe, and think" is essential in observing a situation.

When a player makes an error, misses an assignment, or does something unnecessary, the coach must remind him/herself that the ultimate goal is about creating better people and find a way to address the situation in the best environment possible. For one, if the player does make an error, it's very likely the player is already beating him/herself up over what just occurred. Yelling and screaming at a player who messed up is not going to make the situation any better; however, it may do the opposite and force the player to get inside his/her own head and start second-guessing everything that just happened. In one of my training programs with a young freshman player, he shared a statement that was learned from his mother that resonates in this situation. He said, "When I make an error, the first thing that comes to my mind is 'be here now.'" This saying allows the player to be able to refocus on the present, since there's nothing that can be gained by focusing on the past.

STEP 2: IDENTIFY THE BUTTON

The next step is to be able to have an awareness and understanding of your "buttons" that can be pushed in practice, meetings, and games. People often say, "So and so pushed my button, or this pushes my button." But what most people don't realize is that no one or no thing can push your button unless you allow it to.

For example, let's say you are coaching a tennis match and your player is doing well. It's a tight match and every point matters. However, the chair umpire makes a call that goes against your player, and it puts him/her in a loss for the game. Immediately, you jump to the fence and start screaming at the umpire for the blown call. Your player is also in agreement and starts to join in and before you know it, both you and your player are tossed out of the game, losing the match completely.

Let's go back and see how your button was pushed. The umpire makes a call that you think is wrong, and it upsets you because it has a direct impact on one of your players and results in a loss. You take your frustration out on the umpire, and you get tossed for what you did and said. How was your button pushed? Many immediately reply that it was when the umpire made the bad call. However, the umpire's bad call didn't let your button get pushed. You let your own button get pushed. No one can push your button unless you put it out there and let him or her push it. What the umpire did and said was about him/her. How you choose to interpret the situation is about you. The umpire makes the call to the best of his/her ability. However, your interpretation is that the call is unfair and goes against your player. The umpire has pushed your "it's unfair button."

The pushing of your buttons can also be examined with how you handle situations with your players directly in practice and games. You are now coaching a basketball team during a scrimmage at practice. You spend time working on a certain play that has taken a lot of preparation and effort on your part to work into your game plan. The team keeps practicing this play over and over, yet your point guard is having challenges reading the situation and making the correct throw. After a few minutes of running through the play, you blow your whistle, gather the team together, and start yelling at the player who doesn't seem to get it, belittling him/her in front of the team. Your button was pushed, and every player is aware of the situation.

Again, no one can push your button unless you let him/her. Here's how you let the player push your button. It's obvious a lot of time and energy was spent on your end in developing the play and the focus in practice to getting it done. You interpret the player as being lazy or not taking the scrimmage seriously, and you put your button out there to be pushed. In fact, it's really just the opposite. The player is struggling to figure the play out, but does not know how to ask for help because in the past when he has asked for help, he was embarrassed by you teasing and making fun of him for not knowing the answer. The player has consciously decided not to ask for help because he knows it will only make the situation worse.

STEP 3: RESPOND VS. REACT

There are a couple of ways to handle a situation when your button is pushed. In the two previous scenarios, the coach reacted to the situation. His button was pushed, and there was an immediate reaction to what occurred. Reaction is often based on emotion, generally negative—anger, frustration, annoyance, fear, guilt, and so on. Take a moment and recall those times you've let your button be pushed. Why was it pushed? What allowed you to get it pushed? It was probably something that connected immediately to an emotion, and was a knee jerk reaction to a negative emotion.

Being able to respond to the same situation with positive direction can provide a tremendous difference as to how the person whom the behavior is directed at hears or reacts to it. Responding is based on awareness or a thought process. A coach who is able to respond has the ability to stop, breathe, and think about the most effective way to handle the situation. Most coaches want to encourage the athlete to learn and grow from adversity. They want to provide direction to help them become better. Most individuals, regardless if he/she is an athlete, will handle a coach who responds much better. An athlete does want to improve, get better, and not let their teammates down. When they do mess up, no one on the field feels worse than they do at that moment...guaranteed! Yelling, belittling, and reacting make them feel worse. Taking the time to respond with positive direction will be a much more effective approach.

STEP 4: USE EMPATHY TO MOTIVATE

Once the coach has made the choice to respond, the ability to use empathy to motivate the players is much more appropriate. Empathy is the ability to understand and appreciate the thoughts, feelings, and attitudes of another individual. Coaches at one point or another played a sport. As a player, they certainly experienced moments where they messed up, had an error, or felt they had lost a game for their team. There is no worse feeling for a player than to make an error and know he has let himself, his team, and his coach down. Anyone who has ever experienced that situation knows the isolation, loneliness, and emotional toll it takes. Some players are able to put it into the past, but for young athletes, it is an extreme challenge. It does not do a coach any good to go after that player to motivate or inspire the player in that moment. Players do not want their coach to lose confidence in them or their ability, and knowing they let the coach down feels awful.

In providing positive direction, a coach is immediately able to recall those similar situations in their own playing history and use them to connect with the player on an entirely different level. There are certain life principles that can be used to offer deeper insight into those moments that allow the player to embrace his or her error and learn to grow from them. Comments such as these can be helpful: Challenges are opportunities for growth; There are no mistakes—only opportunities; It's not how hard you get knocked down, but rather how quickly you get back up; Errors provide the opportunity to see just how badly you want to improve.

Empathy allows a coach to also acknowledge and validate the situation for the player and then provide the direction needed to refocus and get back into the practice/game. Using positive direction as a skill in coaching provides a number of opportunities for the coach to be a more effective communicator, the players to be more responsive and listen, and the team to become more united and a stronger unit. Here's an opportunity for you to spend a few moments to identify your buttons, recognize the reasons why you have those buttons, the difference between reacting and responding, and how you can reframe those comments by using empathy.

1. My buttons are/I get really upset when:

    a.

    b.

    c.

    d.

    e.

2. It really upsets me/makes me angry because:

    a.

    b.

    c.

    d.

    e.

3. Reaction statement:

    a.

    b.

    c.

    d.

    e.

4. Empathy/responding statement:

    a.

    b.

    c.

    d.

    e.

INTEGRITY

Integrity is one of those words commonly posted on locker room walls. It is a value most parents want their children to uphold. A person of integrity has a positive core set of values, is able to confront others who seem to make inappropriate decisions, and has a genuine approach. Integrity is often described as the person who is walking down the hallway, sees a piece of trash, picks it up, and places it in the correct trash container. They pick it up, not because someone is watching or telling them to do so, but because it's the right thing to do. A person with integrity is often seen as a leader who always accepts responsibility for his behavior. A coach who has a sense of integrity will often accept responsibility when the team loses and place the loss directly on his shoulders, implying that he did not prepare the team effectively. However, this same person of integrity will shift the focus off himself as the reason when the team wins, and give the credit to the athlete(s) on the field, court, or rink.

Leadership is an important focus of coaches on the field. Coaches often tell players to be a leader with their teammates. There are two basic types of leaders: positive and negative. Most coaches claim to be positive leaders, yet their tactics often stem from a negative approach. Their core values are appropriate, but the manner in which they carry themselves crosses boundaries. For instance, a coach may value excellence, but he may humiliate a player in order to motivate that player in a particular situation. The athlete probably responds to the humiliation, thereby validating the coach's strategy, yet the result could have been the same without the need to embarrass the player.

Most youth coaches rarely receive any type of true training on what it means to be a leader. A youth coach accepts the responsibility of the team, but lacks the necessary skill set for being a leader. The effort is dismissed since it involves youths with minimal accountability. Therefore, the coach is not properly prepared to take on the role.

Carol Dweck, Ph.D. of *Mindset*[2] devotes an entire chapter to the mindset of individuals in sports. She identifies two types of mindsets: growth and fixed. She goes into great detail about mindsets and the impact they have on various situations that occur in an individual's life. A fixed mindset is when people are relatively closed in their thinking. It is their way or the wrong way. When something doesn't go as planned, they blame external factors for keeping them from success. They often place blame on things surrounding them.

A growth mindset is when a person is open to life's challenges. These people are in a constant state of learning and developing. When a person does not succeed, it does not necessarily mean that he has failed; rather, he has created a learning opportunity. A person with a growth mindset is often happier, healthier, and in a much better place when it comes to the numerous obstacles. A person with a fixed mindset believes that he has only a limited amount of knowledge, intelligence, and talent. A person with a growth mindset knows that learning, intelligence, and talent can develop and grow as life experiences and events occur.

When it comes to integrity and leadership, a coach with a fixed mindset believes he already knows what it takes and means to be a leader. He is less likely to admit he can learn from situations. On the other hand, a coach with a growth mindset knows that everyone he meets is both a teacher and a student. He has the desire to learn in any situation. He continues to develop into a leader throughout his life. Dweck encourages the growth mindset and identifies a four-step process:

- Step 1: Learn to hear the fixed mindset voice.
- Step 2: Recognize there is a choice.
- Step 3: Talk back to the fixed mindset with the growth mindset voice.
- Step 4: Take the growth mindset action.[3]

The Bully Culture that exists in sports can certainly benefit from the growth mindset. In order to reduce the amount of bullying that takes place, coaches must look within to determine the most important role for their players. Just because traditions and initiations have taken place does not mean they need to continue. A coach with integrity and a growth mindset can develop new ways to build a sense of team. If the goal of hazing is about creating a strong team, then he must be deliberate in providing team-building activities that are supervised instead. Coaches can break old habits to create the desired results. By focusing his players on integrity, he can create a more accepting team on and off the field.

DETERMINATION

The fourth star is determination. Coaches often question the commitment of their players at some point during the season, in particular when losing is involved. When it comes to a lack of wins, it is common to challenge a player's dedication. Coaches associate losing with a level of determination, rather than a lack of skills.

Significant dedication is required to be extremely successful in sports. Sacrifices are generally made in order to stay committed to a sport. Players know it takes incredible fortitude if they are going to continue playing at a competitive level. It also takes extraordinary willpower to go from playing youth recreation to competitive travel and club, as well as varsity in high school, college D1, and then professional.

Changing the culture in any circumstance requires a well thought-out plan, patience, and persistence. This particular star encourages coaches to be as determined off the field with players as they are on the field. Confronting the bully culture in sports is even more of a challenge. Not only is it likely that the behavior has been present for years, but everyone in the community openly promotes it. A coach puts his reputation on the line in addressing the current norms of the team. However, when coaches and players utilize their focus of determination to help eradicate bullying behavior, then the school communities and student populations will truly benefit from their talents and gifts.

EXCELLENCE

The final star is Excellence, which is subjective. It is different for every coach, player, and parent. There is always a choice in terms of the bar that is set regarding the level of excellence. A commitment to excellence is a common catch phrase in sports. Coaches excel at excellence. A commitment to excellence in sports allows coaches to set goals, thus creating a game plan to achieve them. One of the most important skills of a coach is to recognize a level of excellence and then motivate his players to reach that point. Using excellence goes hand-in-hand with combating bullying behavior. As a coach addresses his players regarding excellence, he can identify the expected level of excellence off the field. By adding the Upstander role to a player's level of excellence, the coach provides the framework for behavior off the field, specifically dealing with bullying behavior. He can establish an Upstander game plan, implementing it to achieve that goal. Since players are already familiar with their own commitment to excellence, they will be able to relate it to behavior off the field.

The Five-Star Coach is a complete coach on and off the field. Each star (Performance, Respect, Integrity, Determination, and Excellence) represents an essential component of being a highly trained and prepared coach. Whether involved with youth recreation sports, middle school travel/club teams, high school athletes, or working with college athletes, a Five-Star Coach is able to create the type of overall program that takes into consideration winning and competition, creating a positive environment, enhancing academic achievement, addressing character development, and using life lessons to ultimately create a more meaningful sports experience. Furthermore, in terms of bullying in sports, a Five-Star Coach is able to set clear policies and expectations, post behavior guidelines, offer appropriate team building exercises, develop a healthy co-existence between winning and losing, identify inappropriate behavior, acknowledge good sportsmanship, and most importantly be a role model who uses positive encouragement.

ENDNOTES

1 Don Miguel Ruiz, *The Four Agreements: A Practical Guide To Personal Freedom*, Hay House Inc Publishing 1997.

2 Carol Dweck, Ph.D., *Mindset: The Psychology of Success*, Ballantine Books, (2007).

3 Carol Dweck, Ph.D., www.mindsetonline.com.

CHAPTER 16

Hey Parents…Let Them Play

*Knowing what's right doesn't mean much
unless you do what's right.*
—Theodore Roosevelt, the 26th U.S. President

In the summer of 1989, the movie *Parenthood*[1] hit the big screen. The movie supports an all-star cast including Steve Martin, Dianne Wiest, Mary Steenburgen, Jason Robards, Keanu Reeves, and a few others. The main character is Gil Buckman (Steve Martin), a father struggling in his role as a parent who coaches his son's Little League team. He is facing challenges in his life and coming to terms with the dysfunction of his own childhood memories.

A scene at the end of the movie begins with Gil speaking with his wife Karen (Mary Steenburgen). He has just reluctantly accepted a promotion at work, and they are discussing a recent baseball game and the possibility of having a fourth child. At the end of the scene, Grandma (Helen Shaw) offers her two cents' worth by using an amusement park ride analogy.

Gil Buckman
I was still high from the Little League game. Isn't that demented? That a grown man's happiness...

Karen Buckman
...depends on whether a nine-year-old catches a pop-up?

Gill Buckman
What if he missed?

Karen Buckman
But he didn't.

Gil Buckman
But he could have.

Karen Buckman
But he didn't, Gil. You threw him a million pop-ups in the backyard. You cut the odds considerably. If you hadn't--

Gill Buckman
But there's three of them, and you want to have four. And the fourth one could be Larry.

Karen Buckman
They're gonna do a lot of things. Baseball's the least of it.

Gil Buckman
And in all those things, sometimes they're gonna miss.

Karen Buckman

Sometimes they won't.

Gil Buckman

Sometimes they will.

Karen Buckman

What do you want? Guarantees? These are kids, not appliances.
Life is messy.

Gil Buckman

I hate messy. It's so...messy!

Grandma

You know, when I was 19, Grandpa took me on a roller coaster.

Gil Buckman

So?

Grandma

Up, down, up, down. Oh, what a ride.

Gil Buckman

What a great story.

Grandma

I always wanted to go again. It was just interesting to me that a ride
could make me so frightened...so scared, so sick, so excited...and so thrilled
all together. Some didn't like it. They went on the merry-go-round. That
just goes around. Nothing. I like the roller coaster. You get more out of it.
Well, I'll be seeing you in the car.

Karen Buckman

She's a very smart lady. Come on, Taylor. Your ears are ready.

Gil Buckman

Yeah, a minute ago I was confused about life. Then Grandma came in with
her wonderful and affecting roller coaster story. And now everything is
great again.

Karen Buckman

I happen to like the roller coaster, okay? As far as I'm concerned, your
grandmother is brilliant.

Gil Buckman

If she's so brilliant, why is she sitting in our neighbor's car?

The movie cuts to a scene with Gil, Karen, and a room full of parents sitting in the audience watching children perform *Snow White* on the stage. The scene opens with Karen holding a video camera taping the show while Gil sits bored and annoyed watching. Their youngest son, Justin, is sitting next to Karen doing his best to watch what is going on up on the stage. Their middle child, a daughter who is playing the role of Dopey, is on the stage being forced by the other dwarfs to wake up Snow White. As that is happening, Justin screams, "Hey they're hurting my sister" and leaps off his seat, crawls out of the row, and runs onto the stage to stop the dwarfs from pushing his sister. Gil and Karen stand there in the audience helplessly calling for Justin to get off the stage, but to no avail. The teacher/director of the show is chasing Justin around on the stage, the parents are taking pictures trying to figure out who he belongs to, some parents are yelling at them that Justin is ruining the play, and chaos is slowly taking over the show.

The camera swings back to Gil as we see him become further stressed, anxious, and overwhelmed by what is going on and the lack of control he has at that time. As he tenses up, we hear the sound of a roller coaster in the background slowly heading up a hill, while Gil seems to be anxiously anticipating what will occur next. Karen slowly moves over to Gil, less concerned, and begins to smile at the situation. The scene builds with the sound of the roller coaster reaching the top. Gil, looking at all of the chaos, is visibly uncomfortable with the ride. He wants to make it stop. Karen is enjoying the ride, smiling through the twists and turns. It looks as though Gil is about to get sick as he rubs his face to make the ride end. He covers his eyes in hopes of being able to block out what is happening, but the roller coaster continues with no end in sight.

Then the "ride" comes to an end. He removes his hands from his face, watching the director chase Justin. The props have been knocked over while the kids on the stage are playing around. Everyone in the room is now laughing. He is able to rid himself of his stress and starts laughing as well. His eyes even begin to water as he sees his daughter putting her costume on Justin, smiling and laughing out loud.

Gil turns to Karen, with tears in his eyes, notices how beautiful she is. He touches his hand on her stomach where the baby is growing. She takes her hand and places it on top of his and they embrace. Life is going to be okay… actually better than okay.

CHILDREN IN SPORTS

Being a parent brings tremendous highs and terrible lows. Regardless of the age of your child, fear, concern, and anxiety often accompany every stage of parenthood and each life experience. For parents whose child chooses to play sports, it can add an entirely different dimension to an already challenging role.

There are numerous reasons why parents support and encourage their children to get involved with sports. For some, it is a basic need to do something physical instead of sitting on the couch watching TV or playing video games. For others, there is a desire to introduce something that was an important component of their lives that they want their child to experience as well. And for some, there's a conscious decision to push their child into sports to ensure some type of monetary gain or professional life experience. Regardless of the reason, nearly 35 million youth ages 8-18 participate in after-school sports. However, there is no "manual" on how to be a parent in sports.

The world of youth sports offers incredible life experiences. The memories that are created last a lifetime. Parents can either enhance these experiences in a positive way or create unnecessary harm. With the increase of adult driven, professionally run youth sports programs, parents are more inclined to invest in these opportunities if their children seem to have a desire to play. Youth sports have gone from backyard games and stickball to high-level competition. Year-round participation is now the norm. Team uniforms are top quality, as players have matching bags, pre-game and post-game wear, and access to the best equipment in sports. Parents are willing to invest thousands of dollars in these programs and provide private coaches and training, seasonal camps, and travel throughout their states to increase the odds of being "scouted" for a college or professional team. This consumer-based approach often places parents in a customer mindset that comes with unreasonable expectations. Just because a parent spends thousands of dollars on a sports program does not guarantee that the result will be positive. This is where the line can be blurred, and the sport goes from being fun and enjoyable to being stressful and overwhelming.

On fields throughout this country, parents are standing in the cold at soccer games 50+ miles from home. They are wandering the sidelines screaming at their children to perform better. Officials are being challenged because of questionable calls while players watch. Parents openly challenge coaching decisions and have no problem confronting a coach directly after a game, regardless of the embarrassment it creates for their player.

> Imagine a warm early evening in May, where the trees are blos-
> soming, there's a gentle breeze and a baseball game is taking place
> on a field behind the local high school. You are sitting off the left-
> field line with other parents enjoying conversation, reminiscing
> about when your children were playing together only a few years
> ago. Stories of wins and losses, trips to all parts of the state, meals
> at random diners between double-headers, and the friends that you
> have made.
>
> It's a freshman baseball game, and the season is winding down.
> There have been some highs and lows, but for the most part, you
> have survived your first year of high school baseball. The opposing
> team is at bat, and a parent stands up and screams at the batter,
> "Keep your arm up! Stay focused! Hit the ball hard!" The first pitch
> delivered is a strike, and the parent yells, "Come on Blue, that wasn't
> even close." The next pitch comes in, and the batter fouls it back to
> the fence. The parent screams again, "What's going on with you?
> Keep your eye on the damn ball. It's not that difficult!" The batter
> returns to the box, steps in, and before he knows it the umpire

screams, "Strike three!" He walks towards the dugout, with his head down. As he walks back, his father throws his hat down in disgust and screams, "F*^@!"

The game continues with a close play at second base. The umpire screams, "You're out!" The third base coach walks onto the field raising his arms in disgust, "You've got to be goddamn kidding me!" The umpire immediately ejects the coach. They exchange words in a heated argument. The coach walks off to his dugout on the first base side. But he's the only adult with his team, so he cannot be forced to leave the field.

As play resumes, the same father from the other team slowly walks toward first base where the umpire is now in position. Everyone watches this parent berate the umpire for the call. He continues, yet no one stops him—not the coach, players, or other parents. The father gets more and more agitated. The umpire just seems to let it go in one ear and out the other. Yet, there are young players on the field watching this transpire.

You decide it is clearly inappropriate and stand up. You tell the father to "please stop." Everyone freezes, looking at you. Thoughts go through your head, but what is taking place is wrong, and no one seems to care. You yell again, "PLEASE STOP!" The father turns around and makes a beeline toward you. As he walks closer, you say in a calm manner, "Listen, just please stop. The play is over, your coach got ejected, let them be."

He stops about 10 feet from where you stand, responding, "Why don't you come here and say it to my face!" The hair on the back of your neck rises, tension fills the air, and now everyone, including the players, umpires, and coaches are watching you. What do you do?

This situation is a true story that took place not too long ago. It was embarrassing and shameful. It needed to stop. Most parents realize that when these types of situations occur, they are completely unacceptable. Yet, they nearly all chose to do nothing about it. It was disappointing that the umpires let it go on and the coach didn't stop it. Mostly, it was upsetting because the parents who knew this man allowed him to represent their school in that disgraceful manner. It was a freshman baseball game with very little meaning, other than allowing these boys to enjoy the game and have some fun.

This situation is not an isolated incident, and it occurs on soccer fields, basketball courts, hockey rinks, you name it. As an old song by DJ Jazzy Jeff and the Fresh Prince once said, "Parents just don't understand." Parents need to think about how their behavior at these games impacts these young players. Whether it is a game of 9-year-olds or a high school varsity game, the way that parents conduct themselves in the stands is a role model for attitudes and behaviors to these players. Schools and teams across the country now have parents signing contracts requesting their understanding and agreement of expected and appropriate behavior in the stands.

When the topic of parents comes up with coaches, it is as if a hurricane storms through. They cannot share enough horror stories with one another. Each coach claims to have worse parents than the other. They match story for story, parent for parent, how they often interfere with their coaching and ability to teach the sport and have the players enjoy the game.

THE MOST IMPORTANT WORDS

I was heading home from a summer baseball tournament with my son recently. He played well, and his team lost a close semi-final game. He seemed content with his effort as we shared our thoughts about the weekend's performance. We made our routine stop at the Wawa, picking up snacks and drinks for our drive home. While standing in line to pay, a number of younger players in uniform were running around. My son leaned over to me, recalling some of the great times we shared over sports. I immediately agreed, recalling the numerous games, tournaments, and trips we had made over the previous eight years.

The moment was short-lived as the cashier shared the amount that was owed. I looked back at those younger players in line, smiling in my heart. I paid, grabbed the bag, leaned into my son, and said, "I just love watching you play." Those words probably meant more to me than him, but he did acknowledge with a simple, "Thanks Dad." It's true; I really do enjoy watching him play. Nothing really gives me greater pleasure than watching any of my children perform. It is something I have said to him since he started playing sports. "I just love watching you play."

Be a spectator. That's the best role a parent can play in their player's life. Be a supporter. Be a positive role model. Say the most important words to your player, "I love to watch you play." Let them know the pleasure you get out of being present, regardless of wins or losses. Encourage them to continue to grow and get better. Challenge them when times get tough to not quit and to work through the obstacles. In the end, after all the games, miles on the car, nights slept in a hotel room, and fast food visits, they will only be a memory.

VALUE-BASED PARENTING

Very few parents actually invest money and time learning the skill sets of a parent. Tens of thousands of dollars are spent on career and professional development, yet minimal amounts on how to be a parent. The irony is that nearly all parents claim they will go out of their way for their children. They will do whatever it takes to support their children. However, they will not commit to learning the necessary tools of how to be an effective parent.

Most parents use a command-control format to their parenting. They set rules, expect conformity to those expectations, and offer consequences when they are not followed. That approach is somewhat effective when the child is under the age of eight. However, as the athlete grows and matures, his needs from his parents also change. As the player enters adolescence, this approach creates resistance, hardening of the relationship, and increases conflict. That warm and wonderful child has become a stranger in his or her own home.

In other situations, parents learn how to parent from their own parents. Although this method may seem worthwhile, the approach is not necessarily efficient. Parenting a child twenty-plus years ago, times were significantly different than today. The techniques that may have worked then do not work with the challenges facing kids today. Most people don't drive a car that is 20 years old or have appliances in their house that long. Why would parenting skills that are 20 years old be any different? It's not logical. It doesn't make sense.

In order to be the most effective sports parent, the first step is to identify your own personal values. Values are at the core of every belief system. They are essential ingredients in figuring out thoughts, feelings, and actions. The values assessment tool that follows identifies underlying needs and motivations. It offers guidance in choices in sports. Parents who do not live their values tend to become hypocritical. They have difficulties connecting with their children. They try to control their teenager only to discover resistance. Living with your values creates a clear set of rules that allow good decision-making. Values can be used to find compatible teams and experiences that support your way of living. They ensure that your child receives the type of coaching and guidance necessary to match your expectations.

PART I

Consider the values listed below. Circle the 10 values that are most important to you as a parent and what you want for your child in sports. Feel free to add your own.

Accomplishment	Discipline	Honesty	Openness
Achievement	Excellence	Humor	Orderliness
Adventure	Flexibility	Integrity	Respect
Altruism	Friendship	Joy	Team Work
Best Effort	Fulfillment	Leadership	Trust
Commitment	Fun	Loyalty	Truth
Community	Hard Work	Memories	Other:
Other:	Other:	Other:	Other:

PART II

For the 10 you circled, pick the top 5 and rank them in order of importance in the left column, with "1" being most important to you and "5" being least. Then in the right column, rate yourself on a scale of 1-10 with "1" being lowest and "10" being the highest in terms of how satisfied you are that you are currently living that value.

VALUE	RATING
1	
2	
3	
4	
5	

Once you have identified your rating on each value, think about what it would take to go up one number in each value. Whether it is a low or high number, there is always the opportunity to improve and grow. It is important for your player's sake that you consider your role in his or her athletic career.

PART III

What will you do to promote these values?

VALUE STATEMENT
1. I will:
2. I will:
3. I will:
4. I will:
5. I will:

Now that you have created five separate remarks, you can now create your values statement. For those who are creative, use your skills and imagination and design a postcard, poster, or computer graphic that captures your values and thoughts. Then post it in an area where you can view it on a daily basis. If you are willing, make multiple copies and keep them around your home or in your car, and most importantly share them with your player. If you are not comfortable with the artistic approach, simply write them down on a note card and refer to them often. Regardless of how you choose to display your values statement, spend time with your player and share it with him. It is important for you to acknowledge why you want your child to participate in sports and what your ultimate goal is for that child.

There are numerous opportunities within sports to share values, regardless of your child's age. For example, the value of commitment and overcoming adversity is often an issue that can be addressed. Baseball players experience disappointment on a regular basis. Professional ballplayers fail 70% of the time at hitting and yet still get paid millions of dollars. Life is full of peaks and valleys, good and bad, but those people who play ball have the ability to learn about the value of persistence. The athletes who play baseball are aware that no class, book, or lecture demonstrates that lesson more than the game of baseball.

Going from a command-control parenting format to a values-based approach allows for better communication. There is a greater understanding regarding the expectations established as a family. Clear values also provide the needed direction for children as they continue their maturity in life. When decisions are explained through a value system, there is less resistance. The more opportunities you have to demonstrate values, the more you increase the chances of planting a seed that will grow on its own.

ENDNOTES

1 *Parenthood*, a film released in 1989 by Imagine Entertainment and Universal pictures.

CHAPTER 17

Get Inspired and Get Moving

It's not the will to win that matters—everyone has that. It's the will to prepare to win that matters.
—Paul "Bear" Bryant, College Football Coach

INSPIRING STORIES

JOHN (JOHNNY) TOKAR

Founder of Athletes Against Bullying

John Tokar knows first-hand what it is like to be bullied and the physical and emotional toll it takes on a student. Looking at him now, you may not believe it, but Tokar wasn't big enough to stand up to his bullies in his beginning years of high school, and in grades 8-10, he faced bullying almost every day.

After being bullied for too long in Grade 10, Tokar knew it was time to stand up to his bullies. To began going to the gym, working out, and eating healthy. The hard work paid off and by the time he was in grade 12, Tokar was big, strong, and named captain of his high school football team. Although he was no longer bullied, there were still students who were being bullied, so Tokar's teachers asked him to walk some of those students home from school. The teachers felt that because Tokar was captain of the football team and influential that his popularity would help keep those students from being picked on by other students. And it worked each and every time. Knowing what it was like to be bullied, Tokar was always happy to help out.

John Tokar grew up in Regina, Saskatchewan, Canada and has been involved in sports since he was 8 years old. After being a star athlete in high school, Tokar went on to play NCAA college baseball for the Division II Minot State University Beavers. A multi-sport athlete, Tokar also played football for the University of Regina Rams and has played competitive hockey since a very young age. Tokar has spent the past four years as head coach for the Regina Midget "AAA" Mets, in the Saskatchewan Premier Baseball League, and has also coached high school football, hockey, and baseball.[1]

DESEAN JACKSON

Professional Football Player

Philadelphia Eagles

Inspired by a Pennsylvania kid named Nadin Khoury, who stood up against bullies, DeSean Jackson spent time on his anti-bullying campaign. Jackson believes athletes can make a huge difference when it comes to stopping bullying.

In many ways, it is the ideal cause for a pro athlete—exactly the right way to use the country's sports-idol worship for the greater good. There are a million great causes, of course. Anybody who raises money to fight a disease or help underprivileged kids is doing a wonderful thing, but athletes are uniquely suited to fight bullying. From elementary school to pick-up games at the Y, athletes command respect from their peers. They epitomize "cool." And if they say bullying is not cool, that resonates. However, to Jackson, sports can make a huge impact on stopping bullying in another way, too. We just have to view sports differently.

Jackson is all too aware of the dynamics and the involvement of parents in sports. Many parents are so worried about teaching their kids how to win that they never teach them how to lose. Jackson doesn't focus on the parents who measure their kids' muscles at birth, have them lifting weights as an infant, and don't let them walk near a Dairy Queen, let alone stop in and have a cone. In fact, he focuses on all of the other parents. He's concerned about how parents tell eight-year-olds to focus on one sport year-round, or when parents switch high schools to get more playing time for their kids or teach them that winning is the most important thing.

DeSean Jackson wants young players to focus on helping their teammates, not beating their opponents. The on-field objective is the same: to excel athletically and try to win. By changing the focus to their teammates, Jackson believes sports would be a much more positive experience.[2]

COLLEGE STUDENT ATHLETES

SUNY Binghamton 2012

Eight student athletes took part in a "No Bystanders" leadership program that aims to curtail cyberbullying and bullying in general. Representing four different sports teams, they worked with more than 50 fifth-graders on two school visits. They offered ways to recognize and combat bullying and also taught the young students the importance of friendship, trust, courage, and leadership. After opening games and discussion, the kids broke into smaller groups and planned and performed skits together. The role-playing and reinforced behavior helped emphasize the message of inclusiveness and caring.

Front and center in the hour-long presentation was sophomore heavyweight wrestler Tyler Deuel, whose blend of brawn and anti-bullying words were an important visual message for the young kids. Joining Deuel were women's soccer players Jamie Holliday, Kerry Sullivan, and Emily Pape, volleyball player Alex Roland, and cross country and track athletes Abigail Elliott, Caitlin Jelinek, and Carly Kiess.

Spearheaded locally by Binghamton University Assistant Athletics Director Kim King, the No Bystanders program offers the following goals:

- Create a principles-based cyberbullying program, promoting positive youth development for fifth- and sixth-grade students.

- Promote the students as leaders within the community.

- Develop a relationship of trust among the student body.

- Create an environment of positive peer pressure through courage, empathy, leadership, and humility by emphasizing virtues in action.

- Increase the principles and awareness of what cyberbullying is and how it affects people within our society as a whole.

- Establish an efficient process to combat cyberbullying.

- Provide students with the necessary resources to combat cyberbullying.

- Create empathy in students so that bystanders speak out against cyberbullying.

- Remove the false sense of power felt in cyberspace.

The program was researched and developed by the State University of New York Youth Sports Institute, located at SUNY Cortland.[3]

THOMAS BROWN

Anti-Bully Expert and Filmmaker

TERRY MARTIN

Superintendent
Zanesville (Ohio) City Schools

Bullying, both in its regular and cyber forms, is a big and growing problem, but combating the abuse may start with something small: an embroidered patch with the letters A.A.B (Athletes Against Bullying).

The brainchild of veteran anti-bullying educator and filmmaker, Thomas Brown and Superintendent of Zanesville (Ohio) City Schools, Terry Martin, A.A.B. asks athletes on participating teams and in school sports programs to sign a pledge not to engage in bullying behavior at home or in school or participate in any form of hazing, and to stand up for the victims of the merciless teasing and tormenting that bullies employ.

After signing the pledge, student athletes receive the official A.A.B. patch to sew on their uniforms, which has been endorsed by the Ohio High School Athletic Association and can be customized to individual school colors.

While wearing team jerseys with the A.A.B. patch, athletes are also expected to educate younger students about the unfairness of bullying others and the harm that it causes.

Brown believes that if the athletic community supported the importance of anti-bullying awareness and did its part to take a stand against childhood bullying, its vast resources, popularity, and influence could actually do something about this ages-old bullying problem. In announcing the A.A.B. program, Thomas Brown challenged the athletic community at all levels to help spread its anti-bullying message: "Together we can actually do something to help those thousands and thousands of children who are terrified to go to school, and possibly avoid further bullying-related youth suicides and shooting tragedies."[4]

PIERRE ANGEL

Founder, Dear Bully Players

Columbus, OH

A local woman's efforts to make a difference in the lives of children in her community inspired her to take on the battle against bullying. Pierre Angel is the founder of Dear Bully Players, an organization founded to help local kids who are victims of bulling. She first volunteered as a basketball coach for children in her local community.

During her time as a coach, her team, the Capital City Mustangs, won a championship, but that trophy was quickly overshadowed when she learned about the bullying occurring among her players. It was that discovery that inspired Angel to begin her organization.

Angel was both bullied and a bully, so she decided to give back when she changed her life. With the help of her assistant, Tasha Watkins, Angel has been able to help students all around Columbus put their experiences into words and then into monologues as a way to turn the tables on their bullies.

Angel hears numerous stories about kids being bullied because of their weight or because of the clothes they wear. She encourages children to spin harsh words into positive words for the bully. Some of the older kids in the Dear Bully Players group have even put together a rap song as a way to connect with their classmates and convey their message about bullying.

She hopes to recruit more students from other Columbus-area elementary schools into the organization so that Dear Bully Players can change the culture of bullying before it begins. If you are interested in learning more about Dear Bully Players or if you are interested in joining, Pierre Angel can be contacted by email at dearbully@gmail.com.[5]

BOSTON VS. BULLIES

The Sports Museum and Boston Sports Community

BOSTON vs. BULLIES is an anti-bullying initiative presented by The Sports Museum and the Boston sports community. It features current athletes from Boston's professional sports teams sharing their stories and providing kids in their community with ways to stand strong against bullying. Current athletes from the Boston Red Sox, Boston Celtics, Boston Breakers, Boston Cannons, New England Patriots, Boston Bruins, and New England Revolution talk about the importance of standing up to bullying and getting help. Kids learn about bullying, the different forms it can take, its hurtful impact, and effective strategies to prevent and stop bullying.

The initiative includes the BOSTON vs. BULLIES website, public service announcements, student programs, and an educational video. It is designed for teachers, youth leaders, after-school program staff, parents, and caregivers of upper elementary and middle school students. It includes key bullying prevention information and strategies that every kid needs to know. The program features interactive activities to get kids actively involved in developing and practicing the skills they need to effectively prevent and stop bullying.[6]

DUANE WEST

Former Professional Football Player

As a child, Duane West was a victim of bullying, with other kids isolating and teasing him. However, he learned to fight back, not with his fists, but with knowledge.

After a stint as a football player for the Florida Bobcats of the Arena Football League, West appeared as a celebrity youth motivator on *The Maury Povich Show*. He now visits schools and communities to inspire young people to lead productive lives.

West is the keynote speaker of the Bound for Greatness Celebrity Anti-bullying, Leadership and Wellness Tour. Through singing, dancing, and audience participation, he addresses issues such as anti-bullying, leadership, and health and wellness. West wants to teach children how to be tolerant, understand diversity, and develop as productive people.[7]

WE ARE ALL DANIEL CUI

Uplands High School, Crystal Springs, CA

Daniel Cui was a high school freshman soccer goalkeeper who struggled with a rough start to the season with a series of blown saves. Some students in the school created a picture album of his efforts on Facebook. However, numerous negative comments were made about his lack of skills, and he became the butt of jokes and the scapegoat for the team's losing record.

Daniel noticed the pictures and remarks. He became sullen, saddened, and depressed to the point that he didn't want to return to school. But what transpired was unexpected and truly inspirational. The whole high school rallied to defend him. After one of his teammates and friends changed his profile pictures to a photo of Cui making a save, more than 100 other students did the same. The posting went viral saying, "We are all Daniel Cui," and with newfound confidence, Cui returned the next season to play the game of his life and lead his team to a win.

Realizing the growing use of technology and cyberbullying, Facebook created Facebook Stories, which highlights situations and individuals who use Facebook in extraordinary ways. You can also Google this story to watch this group of outstanding students.[8]

RESOURCES TO GET STARTED

NATIONAL FEDERATION OF STATE HIGH SCHOOL ASSOCIATIONS

www.nfhs.org[9]

Since 1920, the National Federation of State High School Associations has led the development of education-based interscholastic sports and activities that help students succeed in their lives. NFSH sets directions for the future by building awareness and support, improving the participation experience, establishing consistent standards and rules for competition, and helping those who oversee high school sports and activities.

The NFHS, from its offices in Indianapolis, Indiana, serves its 50-member state high school athletic/activity associations, plus the District of Columbia. The NFHS publishes playing rules in 16 sports for boys' and girls' competition and administers fine arts programs in speech, theater, debate, and music. It provides a variety of program initiatives that reach the 18,500 high schools and over 11 million students involved in athletic and activity programs.

CHANGING THE GAME: THE GLSEN SPORTS PROJECT

www.sports.glsen.org[10]

Changing the Game: The GLSEN Sports Project is an education and advocacy initiative focused on addressing LGBT issues in K-12 school-based athletic and physical education programs. The Sport Project's mission is to assist K-12 schools in creating and maintaining an athletic and physical education climate that is based on the core principles of respect, safety, and equal access for all students, teachers, and coaches, regardless of sexual orientation or gender identity/expression and integrating these efforts into overall school plans to ensure a safe, respectful school climate and culture.

POSITIVE COACHING ALLIANCE (PCA)

www.positivecoach.org[11]

Positive Coaching Alliance (PCA) is a national non-profit with the mission to provide all youth and high school athletes a positive, character-building youth sports experience. Since its 1998 launch at Stanford University by founder and Chief Executive Officer Jim Thompson, PCA has impacted more than four million youth athletes. PCA reaches youth and high school sport leaders, coaches, athletes, parents, and officials through live workshops, online courses, published books and articles, and a series of alliances with nationally recognized coaches, athletes, academicians, businesses, and national youth sports organizations.

ATHLETES AGAINST BULLYING (A.A.B.)

www.athletesagainstbullying.ca[12]

It's no secret that youth are influenced by their peers and even more so by the athletes they look up to. The athletes that make up the Athletes Against Bullying alliance (A.A.B.) realize the importance of using their status and influence as athletes to make an impact on the many youth who are affected daily by bullying. The program is designed for students from elementary school to high school.

OLWEUS BULLYING PREVENTION PROGRAM (OBPP)

www.olweus.org

The Olweus Bullying Prevention Program (OBPP) is the most researched and best-known bullying prevention program available today. With over 35 years of research and successful implementation all over the world, OBPP is a whole school program that has been proven to prevent or reduce bullying throughout a school setting. The OBPP is designed for students in elementary, middle, and junior high schools (students ages five to fifteen years old). Research has shown that OBPP is also effective in high schools, with some program adaptation. All students participate in most aspects of the program, while students identified as bullying others, or as targets of bullying, receive additional individualized interventions.[13]

FEDERAL GOVERNMENT WEBSITE

www.stopbullying.gov

StopBullying.gov provides information from various government agencies on what bullying is, what cyberbullying is, who is at risk, and how you can prevent and respond to bullying. StopBullying.gov coordinates closely with the federal partners in Bullying Prevention Steering Committee, an interagency effort led by the Department of Education that works to coordinate policy, research, and communications on bullying topics. The federal partners include representatives from the U.S. Departments of Agriculture, Defense, Education, Health and Human Services, the Interior, and Justice, as well as the Federal Trade Commission and the White House Initiative on Asian Americans and Pacific Islanders.[14]

SPRIGEO ONLINE APP

www.sprigeo.com

Sprigeo's online anonymous reporting system is born from 30 years of education experience, 3,000 hours of software design, and consultation from school administrators, researchers, psychologists, teachers, parents, and students.[15]

PACER'S NATIONAL BULLYING PREVENTION CENTER

www.pacer.org

Founded in 2006, PACER's National Bullying Prevention Center unites, engages, and educates communities nationwide to address bullying through creative, relevant, and interactive resources. Pacer's bullying prevention resources are designed to benefit all students, including students with disabilities. PACER offers digital-based resources for parents, schools, teens, and youth.

STRATEGIES AND TACTICS: INTERVENTION AND PREVENTION

- Create an environment where your player feels safe talking with you.
- Help player(s) create friendships.
- Listen to what your player(s) is saying and acknowledge and validate it.
- Pay attention to your player's moods.
- Discuss strategies to overcome possible bullying situations.
- Create a school committee with members from community, faculty, administration, and law enforcement and peer leaders.
- Develop and implement rules and consequences.
- Train your staff.
- Offer a bully reporting system—anonymous, if needed.
- Focus on weekly classroom curriculum.
- Increase adult supervision.
- Encourage upstanding behavior.
- Create partnerships with parents/educators/coaches.
- Implement a research-based anti-bullying program.
- Make agreements of expected appropriate conduct with everyone involved with sports (administration, coaches, athletes, parents, officials, spectators).
- Discuss the importance of sports integrity: what it means and how to act.
- Reward positive behaviors.

ENDNOTES

1 http://www.athletesagainstbullying.ca/page/about

2 http://sportsillustrated.cnn.com/2011/writers/michael_
   rosenberg/10/06/bullying/index.html

3 http://www.binghamton.edu/inside/index.php/inside/story/student-
   athletes-teach-anti-bullying-in-grade-schools

4 http://www.momsteam.com/bullying/athletes-asked-stand-up-against-
   school-bullying

5 http://www.winninghoops.com/pages/Breaking-News-Volunteer-
   Coach-Takes-On-Battle-Against-Bullying.php

6 Kim Storey, EdD, Michelle Gormley and Ron Slaby Ph.D., *Boston vs.
   Bullies Facilitator Guide*, 2012

7 http://chronicle.augusta.com/news/education/2011-09-16/
   ex-pro-football-player-preaches-against-bullying

8 http://www.facebookstories.com/stories/1921/video-we-are-all-
   daniel-cui

9 National Federation of State High School Associations.

10 Changing the Game: The GLSEN Sports Project.

11 Positive Coaching Alliance.

12 http://www.athletesagainstbullying.ca/page/home

13 Olweus Bullying Prevention Program.

14 www.stopbullying.gov.

15 www.sprigeo.com.

CHAPTER 18

Call to Action

Often the right path is the one that may be hardest
for you to follow. But the hard path is also the one
that will make you grow as a human being.
—Karen Mueller Coombs, Author, *Bully at Ambush Corner*

The time has come for all of us involved with youth, teens, and sports to do some serious self-reflection. Whether you are a coach, a player, a parent, or a casual spectator, you must begin to focus your efforts on the impact of bullying in sports. Our country has gone on long enough without a national dialogue examining how the culture of sports is created, who promotes it, and what the long-term consequences are. The last exclusive study about bullying in sports occurred over 20 years ago. It's time to create a new national study.

This book was two years in the making. It began with an innocent conversation in September 2011 with Marty Teller, Community Marketing Manager with the Sports Authority in New Jersey, when we discussed the workshops I present on bullying. He immediately offered his storefronts as a location for me to speak. A few months after our initial meeting in the spring of 2012, I presented "Bullying in Sports: What Coaches, Parents, and Players Need to Know." As a result, the International Bullying Prevention Association invited me to speak at their International Conference on November 5, 2012. The title of my workshop changed to "Bullying in Sports: The Injuries We Don't See." I presented to a standing room-only group of nearly 100 professionals. Following my remarks, a line of a dozen-plus people stood waiting to talk with me about my presentation. The most common question asked was, "Where can I get a copy of your book?" I took their names and emailed them saying, "It will be out shortly, and I'll keep you posted when it is available." I immediately returned to my hotel room and started writing this book.

I finished writing in January 2013. In February, I created a GoFundMe webpage, reaching out to family and friends to help promote the self-publishing of this book. I received a significant amount of support validating my efforts. I am forever grateful to those individuals who saw the importance of this work and were there for me from the beginning. As I was set to self-publish the book, I met Traci Totino, the head of TNT Educational Services. Halfway through the explanation of my book, she contacted Lee Anne Fisher at Pearson Education. In December 2013, I finished the author review draft of this book. Sports Authority of New Jersey is now an official partner with me, offering financial support, as well as its locations and coaches' kits to participants who attend my presentations. Pearson Education has used its powerful network to connect me with organizations that are mutually invested in this area. Opportunities continue to present themselves to me each time I share this information with others.

Since I started writing this book in 2012, a number of national sports-related stories have surfaced, all featuring stories with elements of bullying behavior. It began with Chris Culliver's homophobic interview with Artie Lang at Media Day for Super Bowl XLVII, which created a firestorm of negative coverage on football's biggest stage. Then came the Bronx High School of Science boy's track team taking locker room behavior too far and being accused of hazing and harassment. Coach Mike Rice of the Rutgers University Division 1 basketball team was then accused of bullying behavior by an assistant coach who uncovered significantly questionable antics toward players. He was quickly fired along with the athletic director, creating an internal investigation that led to the lacrosse coach being suspended for unacceptable behavior as well. Over the summer of 2013, Ricardo Portillo, a soccer referee in Utah, was killed after being struck by a teenager over a call during a game. The player has since pleaded guilty in juvenile court. Later in the year, the news involved the National Football League and the Miami Dolphins; however, in this case, the accusations of bullying were coming from the target Jonathan Martin toward the bully, teammate Richard Incognito. The NFL and NFLPA have identified lawyers to investigate the situation. Both players have their own lawyers, and the stage is now set to take bullying in sports to the national level.

Bullying in sports today is at the place in the national consciousness where concussions were only a few short years ago. Today, there are protocols at all levels to ensure that our young athletes take care of themselves. My intention is to begin this dialogue aggressively and get others to join me in this campaign. Although bullying is already present on the national stage, this shift focusing on bullying in sports offers a unique opportunity. Not only can we address the behavior by curbing it significantly at its core, but we can also create change in behavior by utilizing the power of sports. I am looking for partners who are involved in professional sports (NFL, MLB, NHL, MLS, Olympics, owners, athletes); companies who provide the gear, equipment, and clothing to athletes (Sports Authority, Nike, Adidas, Under Armour); schools; competitive and recreational teams; universities and colleges; and most importantly, parents who want to help our young athletes compete and play in healthy environments.

Please join me and visit my website at www.bullyinginsports.com. Or follow me on Twitter at @coachrandysays and be a part of positive change in sports.

General Research

Research clearly indicates that bullying is learned behavior and detrimental to the academic, physical, social, and emotional development of all involved—bullies, targets, and the bystanders who witness it. A wave of recent bullying incidents with tragic outcomes has shed a renewed light on this issue. The advent of technology allowing for impulsive, anonymous, and rapid communication has expanded the opportunities for bullying to a degree that necessitates more innovative and immediate responses than ever before.[1]

Bullying research began in earnest with Dr. Dan Olweus, founder and creator of the innovative Olweus Bullying Prevention Program. The research community recognizes him as a pioneer on bully/victim problems, as well as a world-leading expert. (For example, the British newspaper, *The Times*, described Dr. Olweus as "the world's leading authority," and several other international newspapers have described him in such terms as well.) Olweus's leading position is also documented by the fact that he is the most cited Norwegian/Scandinavian researcher in psychology and education according to several independent analyses of citation frequency (the Social Citation Index and the Science Citation Index).

For over 40 years, Dan Olweus has been involved with intervention work in the area of bully/victim problems among school children and youth. As early as 1970, he started a large-scale project that is now generally regarded as the first scientific study of bully/victim problems in the world. (This study was published as a book in Scandinavia in 1973 and in the United States in 1978 under the title *Aggression in the Schools: Bullies and Whipping Boys*.) In the 1980s, Olweus conducted the world's first systematic study on intervention against bullying, which documented a number of positive effects of his "Bullying Prevention Program" (e.g., Olweus, 1991, 1992, 1994; Olweus & Limber, 1999). In 1993, Dr. Olweus published his book, *Bullying at School:*

What We Know and What We Can Do, which has since been published in 15 languages. In the late 1990s, Dan Olweus and his group at the University of Bergen in Norway conducted several new large-scale intervention projects, again achieving good results. One of these studies forms part of an international project on bully/victim problems and features researchers from Japan, England, the Netherlands, the USA, and Norway.[2]

Through the 1980s, Dr. Olweus's work comprised the great majority of bullying-related research. In 1990, GLSEN, the Gay, Lesbian & Straight Education Network, was established, and is now the leading national education organization focused on ensuring safe schools for all students. According to its mission, GLSEN envisions a world in which every child learns to respect and accept all people, regardless of sexual orientation or gender identity/expression. GLSEN seeks to develop school climates where difference is valued for the positive contribution it makes in creating a more vibrant and diverse community.[3]

GLSEN is on the innovative edge in research for LGBT and bullying. Their 2011 National Key Findings Survey identifies significant findings of Lesbian, Gay, Bisexual and Transgender youth in our nation's schools. A significant component of their work and efforts is their powerful program, *Changing the Game: the GLSEN Sports Project,*[4] the first documented effort to connect bullying with athletics. This program is an educational and advocacy initiative focused on addressing LGBT issues in K-12 school-based athletic and physical education programs. The Sports Project's mission is to assist K-12 schools in creating and maintaining an athletic and physical education climate that is based on the core principles of respect, safety, and equal access for all students, teachers, and coaches, regardless of sexual orientation or gender identity/expression, and integrates these efforts into overall school plans to ensure a safe, respectful school climate and culture.[5]

In early 2000, PACER (Parent Advocacy Coalition for Educational Rights) noted increased calls from parents about bullying situations. Founded in 1977, PACER Center was created by parents of children and youth with disabilities to help other parents and families facing similar challenges.[6] By

2006, PACER formed the National Bullying Prevention Center, responding to the demand resources and awareness campaigns. PACER is the founder of National Bullying Prevention Month that is held each October and unites communities throughout the country to raise awareness of bullying prevention through events, activities, and education.

THE COSTS OF BULLYING

There is new research that has identified the costs of not providing appropriate anti-bullying training and awareness programs, *The Cost Benefit of Bullying Prevention: A First Time Analysis of Savings*. This study was prepared by the Center for Health Promotion and Disease Prevention at the Windber Research Institute and was funded by the Highmark Foundation, a private charitable foundation dedicated to improving the health, well-being, and quality of life for individuals and communities throughout the areas served by Highmark Inc.[7] The study is an outgrowth of the Highmark Foundation's ongoing bullying prevention initiative. The research was conducted over a three-year period throughout 49 counties in Pennsylvania. The study meets a specific need for investigation into the cost benefits of investing in bullying prevention programs.[8]

The study's findings identified three impact areas: healthcare, schools, and society.[9] Healthcare cost savings are important because they indicate that bullying is far more than a social issue. The effects of bullying are felt not only in schools, but they also ripple through to the healthcare system as costs mount to treat the health conditions that are related to bullying. School cost benefits relate not only to improved school climate and classroom management, but also to school budgets. When students leave school for any reason, including being bullied, public schools lose revenue from state reimbursements for student enrollment. Bullying prevention acts keep students in school who might otherwise leave because they suffer the pain and humiliation of being bullied and, unable to find relief, resort to alternative placements. Societal cost benefits arise from students who stay in school and become productive members of society, and who find jobs and add to community life instead of draining it by using resources within justice and social service systems. The impact of students who drop out differs from those who leave school early because dropouts do not seek alternate placements to complete their education. Society feels the long-term impact in increased costs.

Not surprisingly, the highest cost benefit comes when schools are equipped to interact and intervene with those who bully.[10] This research and information, which purposefully takes the Cost-Benefit Approach (CBA), as opposed to the Return on Investment (ROI) approach, is extremely important for schools, legislatures, leaders, and anyone who works with youth and teens. It is a brilliant strategy since there are costs involved on numerous sides. The upfront costs of creating an extensive anti-bullying campaign are real and must be understood. However, the costs of not following a research-based approach and simply using the checklist strategy are far more expensive to schools and communities in the long run.

Money is the one consistent obstacle ensuring that our students receive the most relevant support. Whether it is the target of the bullying behavior, the individual who bullies, those who simply stand by and do nothing, or the school or the community itself, there is a significant amount of money spent in dealing with the aftermath of bullying. As for those students who habitually bully, some studies say that approximately 33% will be convicted of a criminal offense in their adult years. A longitudinal study in Norway found that 60% of boys identified as "bullies" in middle school had at least one criminal conviction by the age of 24; 35% to 40% had three or more convictions. "Bullies" were three to four times as likely as non-bullying peers to have multiple convictions by their early 20s. This study only included boys, but similar patterns may hold true for girls.[11] The report, *The Price of Prisons*, states that the cost of incarcerating one inmate in 2010 was $31,307 per year. "In states like Connecticut, Washington State, and New York, it's anywhere from $50,000 to $60,000."[12] It behooves administrators and educators to listen to the experts and invest in the most relevant and significant training early on, thus avoiding these costs to the community later.

Money is by no means the only type of cost incurred by bullying and bullying behavior. The targets of bullying behavior experience an attack on their sense of belonging and status, which often results in low self-esteem. In the most extreme cases, targets have taken out their anger through school shootings or by committing suicide. The costs for therapy and counseling are substantial for a family. In addition, if a bullied student takes matters into his or her own hands, the cost to rebuild schools, lives, and communities can be in the millions. And again, approximately 33% of students who habitually bully will be convicted of a criminal offense in their adult years.

Kids who are bullied can also experience negative physical, academic/scholastic, and mental health issues. They are more likely to experience depression and anxiety, increased feelings of sadness and loneliness, changes in sleep and eating patterns, loss of interest in activities they used to enjoy, and decreased academic achievement (GPA and standardized test scores), and school participation. They are more likely to miss, skip, or drop out of school. These issues may persist into adulthood and can manifest as health problems, greater risk of depression, lower self-confidence, increased challenges with interpersonal relationships, and problems with alcohol, drug use, and self-destructive behaviors. A very small number of bullied children might retaliate through extremely violent measures. In 12 of 15 school shooting cases in the 1990s, the shooters had a history of being bullied.[13]

Furthermore, according to Dr. Dan Olweus, half of the children who are bullied turn into bullies themselves.[14] Since bullying behavior is about an imbalance of power and control, some targets feel as though they have lost their own personal power and control over their lives, they feel they have to take back what they lost, and they begin to bully in turn.

Targets of bullying are not the only ones in this equation who suffer. Kids who bully others are likely to also engage in violent and other risky behaviors into adulthood. They are more likely to abuse alcohol and other drugs in adolescence and as adults get into fights, vandalize property, drop out of school, engage in early sexual activity, be abusive toward their spouses and children, and have criminal convictions and traffic citations.[15] According to an FBI report following Columbine, approximately 75% of students who bully end up in prison.

The cost equated to bystanders is harder to discern. They are silenced by fear that bullies will target them if they speak out. Often, they grow up believing that they are powerless to stop abusive behavior in others. Like other types of behavior, this is reinforced over time, and individuals who stand by and watch others being treated inappropriately grow up and continue to be bystanders in their work environments. Kids who witness bullying are more likely to abuse tobacco, alcohol, or other drugs; have increased mental health problems, including depression and anxiety; and miss or skip school.

There are now significant costs for schools because they are increasingly subject to litigation for failing to provide safe learning environments, and in some cases, they are being held responsible for the suicides and school shootings by students. The costs involved for schools are so dramatic that most insurance companies require some type of policy, training, and awareness workshops in order to be covered. Unfortunately, schools are overwhelmed by a number of components, from the importance of increased test scores, teacher tenure and evaluations, and the other mandated expectations that have grown and changed in the past 50 years. Therefore, these important anti-bullying trainings and programs simply become checklist items and are only covered by the least nominal expense and degree.

Only after a significant bullying incident hits a school do they react to what has happened and begin to rethink their strategies and policies. For example, last year a school district in north New Jersey settled a bullying case for $4 million to a student who had been subjected to ongoing bullying, and was eventually injured to the point where he must spend the remainder of his life in a wheelchair. Most schools, at this point, choose to play the game of "Russian Roulette" in hopes of somehow being just lucky enough that their situation doesn't end up on the front page of the news.

Although a majority of bullying takes place in school, communities and legislatures are realizing that it simply is no longer isolated within the confines of the buildings. Communities must become aware that they have a significant role in confronting and dealing with bullying in every part of town. Bullying behavior exists on the walk to and from school, in recreation departments, churches, synagogues, and at local parks.

It is not the sole responsibility of schools to address bullying behavior. Township leaders and councils must become aware of their responsibilities in this issue, because the effects of bullying are far-reaching, well beyond the schools. Communities where bullying is known to take place lose potential home and business owners who decide they'd rather look elsewhere. Families who experience bullying move away, and given today's technology and social media age, instant information enables people to inform others about their own communities. Bullying forces towns to waste valuable time in tackling a problem that is resistant to change, compromises student academic performance, and creates negative perceptions of the school by the wider community, thus increasing parent hostility.

There are numerous costs involved when bullying goes unnoticed, undetected, and underappreciated. The world of athletics is not immune to this and can potentially be an avenue for solutions. With proper training of coaches, workshops for parents, and increased awareness for athletes, we not only help students who are bullied, but genuinely impact the livelihoods of those who perpetrate bullying. We can additionally help educate those individuals who stand on the sidelines to get into the game and start doing something about the negative behavior they see. By doing so, our schools, recreation departments, and communities can all take a proactive role in decreasing this unwelcome and destructive behavior.

ENDNOTES

1 *DuPage County Anti-Bullying Task Force Model Bullying Policy* (2011).

2 Ibid.

3 http://www.glsen.org/

4 Ibid.

5 Ibid.

6 http://www.pacer.org/about/

7 Highmark Foundation, *The Cost Benefit of Bullying Prevention: A First-time Analysis of Savings*, (2011).

8 Ibid.

9 Ibid.

10 Ibid.

11 Dan Olweus, *Bullying at School: What We Know and What We Can Do* (Oxford, UK: Blackwell Publishing, 1993). OBPP, *TG*, pp. 21–22, *SWG CD-ROM Document 1*, pp. 14–15.

12 VERA Institute of Justice, *The Price of Prisons: What Incarceration Costs Taxpayers*, January 2012 (updated July 2012).

13 http://www.stopbullying.gov/at-risk/effects/index.html

14 www.clemson.edu/olweus

15 http://www.stopbullying.gov/at-risk/effects/index.html